My Business Is to Create

MUSE
BOOKS
THE IOWA SERIES
IN CREATIVITY &
WRITING

ROBERT D.
RICHARDSON,
series editor

My
Business
Is to
Create

*Blake's
Infinite
Writing*

ERIC G. WILSON

UNIVERSITY
OF IOWA PRESS,
IOWA CITY

University of Iowa Press, Iowa City 52242
Copyright © 2011 by Eric G. Wilson
www.uiowapress.org
Printed in the United States of America

Design by Richard Hendel

The University of Iowa Press is a member of Green Press Initiative
and is committed to preserving natural resources.

Printed on acid-free paper

Library of Congress Cataloging in Publication Data
Wilson, Eric, 1967–
My business is to create: Blake's infinite writing / by Eric G. Wilson.
p.   cm. — (Muse books: the Iowa series in creativity and writing)
Includes bibliographical references and index.
ISBN-13: 978-1-58729-990-2, ISBN-10: 1-58729-990-9 (cloth)
ISBN-13: 978-1-58729-991-9, ISBN-10: 1-58729-991-7 (ebk.)
1. Blake, William, 1757–1827 — Criticism and interpretation.
2. Authorship — Philosophy.   3. Creation (Literary, artistic, etc.).
I. Title.
PR4148.A9W56 2011   2010046505
821′.7 — dc22

To Robert D. Richardson, Jr.

Only the hand that erases can write the true thing.
—Meister Eckhart

In my writing I am acting as a map maker, an explorer of psychic areas, a cosmonaut of inner space, and I see no point in exploring areas that have already been thoroughly surveyed.
—William S. Burroughs

No knowledge, no serious contemplation, no valid choice is possible until man has shaken himself free of everything that affects his conditioning, at every level of his existence. And these techniques which so scandalize the uninitiated, whether they be licentious or ascetic, this consumption and consummation of organic and psychic fires—sperm and desire—these violations of all the rules and social conventions exist for one single, solitary purpose: to be the brutal and radical means of stripping man of his mental and bodily habits, awakening in him his sleeping being and shaking off the alienating torpor of the soul.
—Jacques Lacarriere

CONTENTS

My
Business
Is to
Create

Only hours from his death on the evening of August 12, 1827, William Blake, though exhausted from his long struggle against an illness of the liver, could not stop creating. He had spent most of his sixty-nine years making exuberant art, in image as well as word, and his demanding muse would not let him rest. Inspiration yet burned within, in spite of the closing darkness. Blake refused to put down the tools of his craft.

A few days before becoming bedridden, he had spent his last shilling on a pencil. He required it for his final work, a series of illustrations for *The Divine Comedy*. Even though he knew that he wouldn't complete his drawings of Dante's paradise — he was feeble and feverish, with a chronically upset stomach and yellowing skin — he continued to compose. He was bent on inventing until he could move no more.

This last desperate devotion was to a calling that had probably killed him. His lifelong engraving practice had exposed him to noxious coppery fumes damaging to his immune system. Lethal as well as enlivening, his muse, in exchange for genius, had exacted his breath. Blake was art's martyr.

And so, committed to the last to the flame consuming him, his joy outweighing the pain, he continued, as he lay on his deathbed, to sketch, driven to convert, for one final spell, his quick thoughts into lively lines. But his brain soon slowed, beginning its descent into the inevitable dimness, and his competent hand faltered. Now, he believed, was the hour. He would have to leave his configurations of heaven undone. He set his instruments aside, his now-dull pencil and his paper riddled with shades.

Faint, he turned toward those attending him, among whom was his wife Catherine, his faithful partner for forty-five years. He saw her crying. Maybe what happened next was a final surge of affection, or perhaps a desperate hope to make the moment stay. Whatever the reason, Blake's haze cleared. His mind revived. He recovered his pencil and paper, reports say, and exclaimed to her, "Stay, Kate! Keep just as you are—I will draw your portrait—for you have ever been an angel to me." This picture he did complete, though it is now lost.

Now finished and feeling the fatigue return, he again laid down his implements, this time for good. He silently said farewell to his earthly exertions—all those pictures and poems, forged in visionary fury—and relaxed, ready for his flesh's demise. As his consciousness gently waned, he sang hymns of his own design, about the eternal bliss to which his spirit would soon rise. He expired at six o'clock, his lyrics still trilling in his head. Catherine remained calm. Perhaps she believed that her life would change but little; she had once said of her husband, "I have very little of Mr. Blake's company. He is always in Paradise."

Blake's imagination was his Eden. As he wrote to a friend after he became seriously ill: "I have been very near the Gates of Death & have returned very weak & an Old Man feeble and tottering, but not in Spirit & Life not in The Real Man The Imagination which Liveth for Ever. In that I am stronger & stronger as this Foolish Body decays."

Blake had good reason for this celebration; he had since he was a small boy relied on his creativity for his true sustenance. When he was four, he saw God's head in the window. He screamed, but took this sight as a sign of his destiny: to behold undying powers and fashion forms to reveal their energies. A few years later, this visionary prospect was reinforced when a spirit said to him, "Blake, be an artist & nothing else. In this there is felicity."

The youth wasted no time in fulfilling the summons.

Daily drawing his perceptions and reading sacred verse assiduously, Blake trained himself to become a creator, and not in any humble sense. He envisioned himself as a poetic equal of Isaiah and Ezekiel (he would later describe a dinner party with both) and as a visual artist on the same level with Michelangelo (with whom he once conversed) and the German engraver Albrecht Dürer.

There was reason for this boldness. Growing up in a family of nonconformist Protestants who had little use for formal education, the boy was encouraged to follow his genius, no matter how idiosyncratic. He read the Bible often, fiercely, with no regard for doctrine, eventually viewing the scriptures not as an archive of divine directives but as a sublime poem. If Isaiah and Ezekiel could transform their spiritual perceptions into heroic verse, if Jesus could find striking parables for the God within, why couldn't William Blake do the same? Didn't the book of Numbers say that God wanted all of his people to be prophets? Didn't Jesus show what a true prophet is: an authoritative and iconoclastic maker of words?

By the time he was a teenager, Blake was well on his way to composing his own holy works. Complementing his Bible reading with studies in Spenser, Shakespeare, and Milton, he wrote accomplished verse in several genres, showing special aptitude for the brief lyric and the seasonal ode. The poems he wrote between the ages of twelve and twenty-one were published in 1783, in a captivating volume entitled *Poetical Sketches*.

But Blake wasn't only consuming and crafting verse during his teen years. He was also learning art, engraving in particular, under the tutelage of James Basire, to whom he was apprenticed in 1772. Because the sensitive and solitary boy didn't fit in with the other more rowdy apprentices, Basire kindly sent him to Westminster Abbey to draw the statues reposing in the gloomy corridors. There among the stately sepulchers, Blake had more episodes in the spirit world. He saw long-dead monks shuffling through the stones, intoning chorales.

In the abbey Blake learned the Gothic style, with its religious focus, clear lines, intricate detail, and antiquarian feel. His tutelage in this technique resulted in his first engraving of note, *Joseph of Arimathea among the Rocks of Albion*, completed in 1773, during his sixteenth year. The piece, influenced by Michelangelo's *Crucifixion of St. Peter*, shows the legendary figure, thought to have brought the Holy Grail to England, standing on a bleak cliff, with the dark sea behind him, in a pose of melancholy brooding.

These early successes launched Blake into a rich creative life. The man lived to make art, original art, mainly in the medium of a peculiar kind of illuminated book, in which unexpected words and surreal images enter into weird, mutually enlightening conversations. He best encapsulated the driving force of his being in *Jerusalem*: "I must Create a System, or be enslav'd by another Man's; / I will not Reason and Compare: my business is to Create." Such revolutionary production, as Blake knew, required nothing less than a lifetime of work. "To create a little flower is the labour of ages." Without art, the world is nothing: "Degrade first the Arts if you'd Mankind degrade." Through art, one can become God: "Jesus Christ . . . is the only God," and this God is "Man in the Spiritual or Imaginative Vision." Not only a consummate artist, Blake's Jesus is also the creator within each of us, the Christ whose revelation is poetry and painting.

This — and not the four biblical texts — is the "everlasting gospel" of William Blake. All of us are artists *in potentia*, and when we bring to fruition our imaginations, we convert the fallen earth into a paradise where the human virtues flourish: love and charity and forgiveness.

Living is creating, and conforming is death. "The imagination . . . is the Human Existence itself." Why is imagination, why is creation, so vital for Blake, essential for becoming human? What is imagination? What is creation? How do we create? Blake had answers for these questions both in word and deed, answers that serve as powerful teachings for accomplished writers and aspiring ones.

In a Harlem apartment in 1948, some years before he would become the foremost poet of the Beat Movement, Allen Ginsberg, twenty-two years old, was relaxing in bed, languidly masturbating, and reading Blake's *Songs of Innocence and Experience*. The young man was suffering a psychological crisis, serious enough to put him in a mental hospital, and he was solacing himself with a combination of auto-eroticism and visionary poetry.

Soon after climax, Ginsberg heard a strange voice. He first took it to be God's, but then concluded that it was that of William Blake himself. It was reciting "Ah, Sunflower," one of the poems of experience, which contains these lines:

Ah Sun-flower! weary of time,
Who countest the steps of the Sun:
Seeking after that sweet golden clime
Where the traveller's journey is done.

In the intonations of the dead poet now alive, these words on the longing for light resonated with Ginsberg; they animated his soul, and transported it to a paradise enduringly solar. He felt, for the first time in months, vibrant, as though the eternal currents of life, bright effusions of the divine, were vitalizing his every fiber.

Communing with the potency that had inspired Blake, his hero, Ginsberg flowed over with enthusiasm. He rushed out to the fire escape and rapped on his neighbors' window. When it slid up, he shouted, "I've seen God!" The glass quickly closed. Then, still hoping for sympathy, Ginsberg called his psychoanalyst, collect, on the pay phone. The doctor refused the charges. His excitement undiminished, Ginsberg hurried back to the apartment and pulled from the shelves one visionary volume after another — Plato, St.

John, Plotinus — and discovered that he now possessed fresh sight. "I was able to read," he reported later, "almost any text and see all sorts of divine significance in it."

Ginsberg later called this episode — a galvanizing concurrence of the erotic, the poetic, and the spiritual — his "Blake Vision," and claimed that it disclosed to him his calling: to be himself a revelatory poet, ripping away veils of prudery and hypocrisy to show the sacredness of *all* existence, sex as well as religion, body and soul alike, the mole in addition to the eagle. Based on his epiphany, he and Jack Kerouac proclaimed their "new vision": "Since art is merely and ultimately self-expressive, we conclude that the fullest art, the most individual, uninfluenced, unrepressed, uninhibited expression of art is true expression and the true art."

Blake affected several other writers in a similar way, stoking their spirits, their locutions, and, sometimes, their loins. ("Energy," Blake wrote, "is Eternal Delight" — and not just intellectual energy: *all* energy.) This list of literary Blakeans is august. It includes Swinburne, Yeats, Dylan Thomas, Aldous Huxley, Hilda Doolittle, Kathleen Raine, Charles Olson, Robert Creeley, Alicia Ostriker, Salman Rushdie, J. G. Ballard, and science fiction writer Philip K. Dick. But Blake impacted other kinds of artists as well: painters like John Ruskin, Dora Carrington, and Joe Coleman; composers such as Ralph Vaughan Williams and Benjamin Britten; pop songwriters such as Jim Morrison, Bob Dylan, and Patti Smith; filmmakers like Derek Jarman and Jim Jarmusch; and underground graphic artists like Alan Moore and R. Crumb.

Blake encouraged all these creators to throw off oppressive traditions and follow their most personal experiences and desires, the more radical the better. The self-reliant voice is the muse of true work, original art. Accompanying this idea of singular creativity, *sui generis*, beyond imitation, is often a celebration of spontaneity, authenticity, naturalness. For many, these characteristics are the markers of a composition's brilliance. In contrast, pieces that appear to be derivative or studied or ornate are frequently deemed inferior. This distinction has almost become common sense: originality equals genius; imitation is mediocrity. As a quick amazon.com survey of writing handbooks shows, innovation has basically become synonymous with art itself.

But what does it mean to be creative? Isn't it possible that "creativity," like "love" or "beauty," has been used so often and in so many contexts that it's dissolved into nebulousness? When we hear the word, we might get a vague, warm feeling. We might imagine solitary, poverty-stricken artists struggling to forge things not yet seen in the universe. We might see a woodland poet scribbling poems as freely as a cardinal tweets its notes. But when asked to define creativity, we're hard pressed and likely to just toss out other hazy generalities, such as "inventiveness."

The term *is* fuzzy, of course, but we should try for clarity. Blake would certainly have us do so, and with extreme specificity. He believed that "To Generalize is to be an Idiot; To Particularize is the Alone Distinction of Merit."

—————

Blake was convinced that "Without Contraries is no progression." He devoted his days not to tranquility but "Mental" warfare. With life, so with art: Blake's printing technique required that he figure his words and images backwards on copper plates, and so his compositions were conflicted, tense gatherings of opposed directions.

Given this antagonistic bent, Blake couldn't let himself view creativity as a simple matter of nonconformity, spontaneity, or naturalness. For him the creative is much more vexed and spirited, a dialectical site where powerful polarities collide, coincide, and merge only to challenge each other once again, perpetually. True imagination flourishes in combat.

Blake's most prevalent antinomies come quickly to

mind: memory and inspiration, innocence and experience, particular and general, energy and form, imagination and reason. On the surface, it seems that the oppositions might fall easily into ranks: surely innocence is better than experience, and imagination, for a poet, superior to reason. However, when we look deeper, we find that the poles are vitally interdependent. Let us take, for instance, inspiration, one of Blake's primary terms for creativity, and its dependence upon memory, tradition.

This is the great problem for all who wish to create: how to transcend a past, both personal and cultural, that has shaped one's habits of perception. Even if there are such things as innate ideas — and Blake believed there were, once saying that man is "Born like a Garden ready Planted & Sown" — history still informs the development of these concepts. A garden is bound by its climate. Blake himself accedes this point when he writes, "As a man is So he Sees," suggesting that one's character, at least partially formed by environment, delimits his vision.

Blake's term for how the past determines the imagination is "ratio." In "There Is No Natural Religion," he claims that "ratio" is inseparable from empiricism, the theory that we know the world through our senses. Scientists since Francis Bacon and Isaac Newton have embraced this theory, maintaining that we establish physical laws through observation. The primary method of observing is induction, reasoning from particular to general. In this model, an experience is only valid, only meaningful, if it relates to a pre-established general category, if it corroborates or revises an authenticated scientific conclusion. Any encounter that can't be connected to an idea that the collective holds true is insignificant, no matter how ravishing. Banished from this empirical realm are all of our exquisitely intangible intuitions and those uncanny glimpses of the soul's striving: the epiphany during the sun-drenched dawn after the ice storm, when the world is aflame; the omen, on a day of long-awaited homecoming, of a sudden abundance of robins.

Scientists might through years of study agree that a certain number of recurring traits make a robin, a robin. The scientific definition of the robin, necessarily abstract, shapes how the culture perceives birds possessing some or all of the semantic characteristics. When an individual schooled in this typology sees such a feathery thing, he immediately, often without thinking, matches the creature to the pre-existing concept of "robinness." Any portion of the fowl that doesn't correspond is ignored. This is the result of the societal ratios that constitute "common sense."

The "ratio" melds the present to the past. It dwells with the "Daughters of Memory." It can be, when too doggedly held, deadly, flattening metamorphosis to monotony. Newton can become the nemesis, more satanic than an imp.

In Blake's eyes, when the "Philosophic and Experimental" prevail, that is, when empirical principles hold sway, everything stands still, dies, and all we do is "repeat the same dull round over again." Blake's description of this redundancy and his liberation from it is striking. He claims that when he witnesses the sun, he doesn't apprehend a disc that resembles a "Guinea" (a coin) but rather "an Innumerable company of the Heavenly host crying, 'Holy, Holy, Holy is the Lord God Almighty.'" The guinea sun is the average perception; if all human encounters with the sun were gathered and classified according to similarity, then the average would be a hovering disc. To waiver from this mean, to catch sight of angels, is to be labeled foolish or insane.

Not only retrospective, the ratio is narcissistic: "He who sees the Ratio only sees himself only." Adhering to the ratio—which can be made up of personal biases as well as those of the collective—one can't look beyond a mirror composed of all he's formerly learned. This reflecting glass expands and surrounds and encloses, becoming a solipsistic prison: shut off from the sun, repeating with the same reflections, stale with despair.

Blake's fear of retrospective, egocentric seeing, of his tendency to fixate on memories of encounters with the material world, sometimes made him go to extremes, as when he demeans nature: "Natural Objects always did & now do

Weaken deaden & obliterate Imagination in Me Imagination is the Divine Vision not of The World nor of Man nor from Man as he is a Natural Man but only as he is a Spiritual Man Imagination has nothing to do with Memory."

Blake made other such pronouncements against nature, like when he criticized Wordsworth for overvaluing matter and memory, but he also, and more frequently, viewed the particulars of the visible world as points of luminous infinity.

To break the ratio and experience particulars, inexhaustibly intricate, evanescent, unpredictable, alive: who can do this? Only the person who holds to his own perceptions, no matter how strange, however far they diverge from the mainstream. He might well witness a solar heavenly host or Ezekiel meditating near an elm. He would be a poetic genius, near to the overwhelming fullness of the cosmos: "He who sees the Infinite in all things sees God."

Blake knew the difficulty of holding this vision. Once, when he was eight years old, he was walking through Peckham Rye, a rural spot in London, and saw "a tree filled with angels, bright angelic wings bespangling every bough like stars." When he returned home and reported this sight to his parents, his father threatened to thrash him for lying. Only the intervention of Blake's mother—who had earlier flogged him for saying that he had indeed witnessed the prophet Ezekiel under a tree—kept him from the beating.

Blake continued to have revelations like this throughout his life: of angels, of prophets, of God. These visions, not surprisingly, incited societal censure. Many followed his parents in refusing to believe in his spiritual perceptions. They called him a liar, or mad. No wonder Blake suffered "Nervous Fear."

But Blake never fully succumbed to his paranoid terrors. He turned always, as an artist would, to the nonjudgmental things of the world. He embraced them, almost amorously, and the more intimate he became, the more expansive his beloved objects grew.

For Blake, extreme closeness exposes the unbounded. We apprehend the infinite not through aloof contemplation but only when the "doors of perception are cleansed." This purification is dependent upon an increase in "sensual enjoyment"—vital attention to minute particulars. Energetic seeing reveals the world in all of its detail, in its variety, its interrelatedness, its depths. Washed free of abstractions, the eyes can witness the "World in a Grain of Sand," or realize that every "Bird that cuts the airy way / Is an immense world of delight."

Imagination for Blake doesn't supplement or supplant what we actually witness, doesn't add wings to a horse or replace a dove with an angel. Imagination apprehends and depicts the world's illimitable fecundity. It is a way of knowing as well as a mode of expression. In his description of his *Vision of the Last Judgment,* a painting now lost, Blake makes this point. Imagination, which he also calls vision, is an immediate perception of reality. Fable, synonymous with allegory, is based on a memory of a past experience that expresses an abstract idea. "Fable or Allegory," he tells us, "is a totally distinct and inferior kind of Poetry. Vision or Imagination is a Representation of what Eternally exists Really and Unchangeably. Fable or Allegory is Form'd by the daughters of Memory. Imagination is surrounded by the daughters of Inspiration, who in the aggregate are call'd Jerusalem." He goes on to say that the "Hebrew Bible & the Gospel of Jesus are not Allegory, but Eternal Vision or Imagination of All that Exists."

Imaginative works are not imitations of existence as it appears to the masses, as it supports common sense. Instead, visions formed by imagination are radically individualistic, unbound by conventional concepts. Indeed, what signals imaginative seeing and saying is irreducible particularity—particularity so resistant to collective conceptions that it is incalculable, inexplicable, unfathomable. "Singular & Particular Detail is the foundation of the Sublime." In contrast, generalizations are the "plea of the scoundrel hypocrite and flatterer."

Think of Ray and Charles Eames's short film of 1977, *The Powers of Ten*. In this nine-minute piece, the camera initially takes an overhead shot of a man and a woman resting on a blanket. The frame is one meter in area. Then the lens zooms outward to cover ten meters, or one to the tenth power. We now see that the couple is picnicking in a park. The camera continues to pull outward, pausing every ten seconds at a new power of ten. The lens doesn't stop until it reaches ten to the twenty-fourth power, the very boundary of the observable universe, one-hundred-million light-years from the picnickers. At that limit, we perceive black space broken only by miniscule bright points.

The camera then makes its way back to earth. Once it reaches the ground, it starts its interior path, penetrating the intricacies of matter. The lens descends until it achieves a magnification of ten to the negative-sixteenth power. As the camera nears its final destination at the edge of a single proton, .0001 angstroms from the picnicking couple, we realize that the insides of the atom resemble the expanses of space, and that the proton itself, the smallest known bit of matter, teems with color.

Whether we travel to the boundaries of the galaxy or to the shell of the proton, we understand: the more specific, the more boundless. The minute is the massive. The sublime shines in the sliver.

This insight stunned Aldous Huxley during his famous experiment with mescaline. On a sunny May morning in 1953, Huxley ingested four-tenths of a gram of the psychedelic drug. Not long after, once the narcotic had taken effect, he did not witness what he had expected—those visions detailed by great seers of the past, such as Blake himself, visions of "many-colored geometries, of animated architectures, rich with gems and fabulously lovely, of landscapes with heroic figures, of symbolic dramas trembling perpetually on the verge of the ultimate revelation."

Instead, Huxley while under the influence experienced idiosyncratic sights growing from his own personal habits and his immediate environment. Sitting in his study he focused on a small vase containing three flowers: a pink rose, a carnation colored magenta, and a purple iris. Before his eyes the flowers exploded through the accumulated ratios and shined in their unprecedented individuality. There they were, what they were, and nothing else, "naked existence," and there was Huxley, "seeing what Adam had seen on the morning of his creation": "Is-ness," the "Istigkeit" of the mystic Meister Eckhart.

This, Huxley thought, was pure being, not, as Plato had it, a "mathematical abstraction of the Idea," but "the pressure of significance" that charged these entities with "their own inner light," set them "quivering" in their occurring. Clasped to his beloved ratios, Plato, in Huxley's mind, "could never have perceived that what rose and iris and carnation so intensely signified was nothing more, and nothing less, than what they were—a transience that was yet eternal life, a perpetual perishing that was at the same time pure Being, a bundle of minute, unique particulars in which, by some unspeakable and yet self-evident paradox, was to be seen the divine source of all existence."

Composing his book on this and related mescaline epiphanies, Huxley realized that he had in fact, in his own inimitable way, enjoyed a moment worthy of Blake, though not as he believed he would. A true Blakean experience, he understood, doesn't involve dreamy fantasies of heavenly delights but intense perceptions cleansed of prefabricated ideas. He duly titled his little essay *The Doors of Perception*, drawing from Blake's lines about the connection between electrified sensuality and spiritual revelations.

Doing so, Huxley, like Ginsberg his contemporary, released Blake's spirit into the sixties counterculture, placing the poet's presence at the center of momentous events: the development of the Esalen Institute, the Big Sur pastoral retreat devoted to Huxley's Blake-inspired exploration of human potential; the emergence of The Doors, Jim Morrison's apocalyptic rock band (desperate to "break on through to the other side") that took its name from Huxley's book; and all the psychedelic quests for hippie enlightenment, brilliantly studied by Alan Watts in *The Joyous Cosmos* and encouraged by Timothy Leary, Ken Kesey, and Richard Alpert, who is now called Ram Dass.

Blake didn't require the sublimely rugged vistas of the American Pacific or Dionysian rock rhythms or dissolved grams of mescaline to facilitate his visions. He needed only his remarkably clear eyes, artist's eyes, and his passion for burning away the surfaces to reach the infinite inwardness, the boundless outgoing. With these enkindled optics, Blake could discern distinctions and unities unseen by most. To perceive and to render the world's subtly divided yet secretly concordant configurations were the primary imperatives of his art. As he once reminded himself, "Leave out this line [,] and you leave out life itself; all is chaos again." "Precision of pencil" was his imperative. For him there was either "Outline" or "Nothing."

Blake's adversary is Newton, prince of abstraction, number over numinous. For Blake, Newton's science, like all empirical undertakings, doesn't get close to physical reality but in fact divorces us from it. The universe of Newton, remember, is composed of indivisible atoms moving through the void with mathematical precision. The essence of this cosmos is the numerical, quantity, abstraction devoid of sentience and warmth. To endorse this cosmology is to trade things for thoughts. In *Milton*, Blake renounces Newton for perversely championing the "Not Human" by donning the "rotten rags of Memory," the decayed trappings of "Rational Demonstration."

Blake would agree with Alfred North Whitehead, the twentieth-century philosopher who challenged "the fallacy of misplaced concreteness." As Whitehead argues in *Science and the Modern World*, the cardinal error of scientific empiricism is mistaking the abstract for the concrete. This mental flaw involves mistaking a *theory* of how things are for how things really are. For instance, traditional science has assumed that "simple location," only an idea, really exists. Scientists believe they can understand a unit of matter as though it were divorced from its environment and moving, without hindrance, across temporal and spatial grids. In reality, though, material forms are inseparable from their surroundings and determined by countless external relationships.

The novelist Walker Percy elaborates on the dangers of misplaced concreteness in "The Loss of Creature." He fears the flight of reality that occurs when events are turned into "examples of" theories. This happens often: in biology classes when students dissect a frog to study not this olive-green mottled corpse but general anatomy; in English literature courses when the class reads a Shakespeare sonnet not as a specific emotion delicately rendered but as an instantiation of the genre. The creature is lost in concept. The real disappears into vapor.

Imaginative perception—dissolving memory into novel solutions, transforming prefabricated givens into unrepeatable ardors—entails intensely looking at the world with love in the heart. When we are imaginative we behold events generously, be they texts or living textures, with a passion for escaping egocentric reductions and exposing ourselves to each being's concreteness. When this happens, what appears is not a mere reflection of our narcissistic dreams, our most personal ratios, nor is it extreme otherness, data seemingly unconnected to the perceiver—the collective constructs of science, the abstractions of empiricism. Rather, what shines is an effulgent copiousness that reciprocates the seer's bounteous affection, granting him the magnificent beauty he desires.

"I know," asserts Blake, "that This World Is a World of Imagination & Vision I see Every thing I paint In This World, but Every body does not see alike. To the eyes of a Miser a Guinea is more beautiful than the Sun & a bag worn with the use of Money has more beautiful proportions than a Vine filled with Grapes. The tree which moves some to tears of joy is in the Eyes of others only a Green thing that stands in the way. . . . [T]o the eyes of the Man of Imagination Nature is Imagination itself. As a man is So he Sees. As the Eye is formed such are its Powers."

"*Esse est percipi*," to be is to be perceived—so Northrop Frye condensed Blake's most cherished idea. Our moods and our beliefs dictate how the world will appear. We *make* creatures as much as we find them. A person who wishes for nature to rise precisely to his most petulant desires will shrink it to a tiny mirror in which he sees only his pettiest parts. Likewise, a man who wants total control of nature will reduce it to indifferent atoms moving like cogs in a ma-

chine, and matter will appear to him that way. But someone who wishes to connect affectionately with nature—
to go beyond his small concerns as well as his communal
inculcations—will witness sublime irradiations, large and
marvelous brightnesses. It's not which vision is true; it is—
which is more alive.

Perceptions exist between subject and object. This is of
course true of all sensory apprehensions. Blake the visual
artist tended, though, to focus on sight. What we sense, with
our optical apparatus, is *there*, real, a palpable event; what
we perceive, with our temperamental mind, is *here*, also real,
a phenomenon of the imagination. The physical world is a
blur of lustrous color. We impress upon these hues meaningful patterns—some genial, some mean. The melding of
colors and forms, shimmers and moods: this is the perception. As Blake writes, "Where man is not, Nature is barren."
Meaning is human. Nature has no meaning. The choice is
ours. We can make the world signify as tepid exhalations of
our cowardice or as monstrous metallic bits. Or, conversely,
we can imbue the cosmos with voluminous blooming.

I and Thou is Martin Buber's lyrical essay on the value of
connecting to the world as a "thou" and not an "it." In perceiving a thing as an "it," one objectifies the entity, turns
it into something distant, alien, cold, a unit of indifferent
matter to be measured and marshaled. But when you apprehend a being as a "thou," you focus on the intimate relationship between you and the creature, on your interdepen-
dence, on how you are meaningful to the creature and the
creature to you. You acknowledge the presence, whether the
being is human or not, as a living agent—complex, paradoxical, tragic, lovable.

Buber exemplifies this distinction by noting linguistic
differences. In the English language, we say of a thing that
is distant, "it is far away," a certain quantity of space from
where we now stand. This way of representing illustrates the

"it" mentality. In contrast, in the Zulu tongue, distance is signified by a phrase that means "where one cries, 'mother, I am lost.'" Here is the world elevated from bland coordinates to the fullness of drama, a stage on which every event is charged with emotion, pregnant with multifaceted and superabundant significance.

As with Blake, so with Buber. Every experience is a decision, a context we create that shapes the world one way or another: atom or bloom, it or thou. Of course we must sometimes of necessity reduce our environment to an "it." We need to get to places on time, have our cars repaired, and secure medicines for our children's ailments. But to do this always is to commit epistemological suicide, to flatten the burgeoning universe to a massive heap of lifeless objects. To live, to thrive, we must more frequently choose to make the earth a "thou," an enduring call for generosity, responsibility, affection.

To transmute the "it" into the "thou," the material into a multifarious vortex, perpetually spiraling, changing, relating to itself and its energetic environment: this is the source of artistic brilliance. William James once said that "[g]enius, in truth, means little more than the faculty of perceiving in an unhabitual way." Emily Dickinson would agree. "My Business is Circumference," she claimed, and by this she meant, among other things, that she reveled in continually churning or chronically concentric perceptions, in the ecstasy of looking at an event from an infinite number of angles and distances. A deliberate stance, a decision to infuse nature magnanimously, this circumferential business dashes staid habits and effects fresh perspectives. It's no wonder Dickinson also wrote: "I Dwell in Possibility / A fairer House than Prose." This abode features numerous windows and superior doors.

If the writer is going to see in the Blakean fashion, by destroying ratios and lovingly exposing the eyes to the light, then she must learn to look, look, and look some more, as closely as possible, and selflessly, too, with an ardent urge to make each observation different from the last and adaptable to the next.

"Damn braces. Bless relaxes." So Blake advises. Do not perceive through overly judgmental eyes, prone to damnation. If you do, you are constrained to witness nothing but your notion of perfection, either fulfilled or violated. Gaze at life rather as though you were always blessing it, consecrating it, humbly, as holy, and then your biases will be relaxed and your curiosity will be aroused and, surprise: there, in your peripheral, a glimmer after which you go, and it is gone, but its absence gleams.

Emerson knew how to do this, and tried to teach his readers: "Turn the eyes upside down, by looking at the landscape through your legs, and how agreeable is the picture, though you have seen it any time these twenty years!" Whitman also could relax decorum, spending hours loafing at his ease, reclining with no expectation of anything, and observing a "spear of summer grass."

Here's what these poets might have you do. Look at the same oak in the morning, in the noon, in the evening. Spin until you're dizzy, and then cock your head at the rushing clouds. When you're going on little sleep, or suffering a slight fever, study your hand: how weird it is. Always keep a notebook with you, and jot, quickly as you can, your sudden impressions, and then comment on them later, and then later on, comment on your comments. Put on sunglasses or get a magnifying glass. Close your eyes for five minutes, and then open, as widely as you can, your lids.

If you can't see something new under the sun, your writing becomes dead or blocked. When the words are coming too easily, you're just replaying old, moldy scripts. When the sentences come not at all, you're darkened by an opaque idea.

Lollygagging or muzzled, shock yourself out of your optical complacency. As H. G. Wells once said, "If you are in difficulties with a book, try the element of surprise: attack it at an hour when it isn't expecting it."

There is an obvious problem: can anyone, even Blake, ever escape the ratio once and for all? The answer is no. Language itself, a system that reduces lubricious events to stable definitions, is ratio, perhaps the most pervasive and potent one of all. The instant Blake composes a verse, no matter how ostensibly original it might be, each word is necessarily limited by its semantic history. The same is true of images: no matter how strange his painting, his pictures can only be meaningful if they relate to an established visual lexicon.

In *Pilgrim at Tinker Creek*, Annie Dillard describes the luminescence of concrete vision and the near impossibility of attaining it. Marius von Senden in *Space and Light* tells stories of people born blind suddenly gaining, through the surgical removal of cataracts, their sight. Citing these accounts, Dillard considers perception freed of signification. Before their liberation from darkness, the blind were unable to connect image with word. Because of this, when they became sighted they experienced, as von Senden puts it, "pure sensation unencumbered by meaning." One patient saw only "different kinds of brightness." Another witnessed an "extensive field of light, in which everything appeared dull, confused, and in motion. He could not distinguish objects." Still another encountered "nothing but a confusion of forms and colours."

These episodes can of course be, as Dillard says, "tormentingly difficult." But they can also be exhilarating, since each phenomenon is to these freshly sighted visionaries "a dazzle of color-patches." When the doctor removed the bandages from one girl's eyes, she walked into a garden and saw a "tree with lights in it." Dillard wishes she could view nature so directly, innocently, like a child not yet burdened by words. She finds, though, much to her chagrin, that she's "been around too long. Form is condemned to an external danse macabre with meaning." She can't "unpeach the peaches."

But unpeaching the peaches, if it were possible, would result in ignorance of a kind, and lack of articulation—no poetry, no philosophy, no knowledge of Milton's architectonics or Blake's turbulent concords. In "Funes the Memorious," Jorge Luis Borges tells the story of Ireneo Funes, a boy from Uruguay who remembers everything in bewildering detail. He cannot understand why a "dog at three fourteen (seen from the side) should have the same name as the dog at three fifteen (seen from the front)." So attuned is he to minutia that his "own face in the mirror, his own hands, surprised him every time he saw them." He "could continuously discern the tranquil advances of corruption, of decay, of fatigue. He noted the progress of death, of moisture. He was the solitary and lucid spectator of a multiform world which was instantaneously and almost intolerably exact." Even the "ferocious splendor" of Babylon, New York, London are pallid in comparison to the "heat and pressure" of Funes' recollections."

This oppressive existence cannot be lightened because Funes was "almost incapable of ideas of a general, Platonic sort." He simply couldn't comprehend why "the generic symbol dog embraced so many individuals of diverse size and form." Incapable of rising from particular to general, he "was not very capable of thought." "To think," after all, "is to forget differences, generalize, make abstractions. In the teeming world of Funes, there were only details."

Like Borges, Blake is aware of the necessity of conforming to collectively held abstractions, shared meanings, prior models. He understood that the past, with all of its memories and ratios, is required for art: "The difference between a bad Artist & a Good One Is the Bad Artist Seems to Copy a Great Deal: The Good one Really Does Copy a Great Deal."

Blake most mimicked that great repository of tradition, the Bible, and the life of Jesus in particular. As we know, Jesus was for Blake a poet of the highest order, who created his own system so he wouldn't be enslaved by another and in so doing revealed the God within us all: creative imagination. But Jesus's poetry didn't come from nowhere; it was firmly based on the Jewish law. The Nazarene himself claimed that his goal wasn't to abolish the law but to "fulfill it." How could Jesus be both iconoclast and culmination? How could Blake, grounded in the prophets and Jesus, be the same?

Jesus epitomized climax and transcendence through a kind of allusion, ironic in nature. He both affirmed the Hebrew law and criticized it, suggesting that the law is valuable but not yet complete and that he is the one to perfect it. This mode is revisionary, taking a prior vision and recasting it in a new and better form. For Jesus, this type of revision involved transferring the law from outward behavior to inward rectitude. The true law is written not on stone but in the heart. Celebrating tradition while surpassing it, Jesus encourages his followers to do the same to their own institutions (even those growing from his words)—to strike an ironic stance, to consider canons as serious powers and to reject them as limiting factors, to mock them and condone them at once.

Memory and inspiration conspire. We can't reject entirely the backgrounds that made us who we are, but unquestioned adherence leads to the "same dull round." We must find a middle way between the retrospective abstractions required for thinking and the perceptions, always now, that explode open clearings never yet seen. The problem arises when we take memory's abstractions *too* seriously, as though they are the sole elements of knowledge, or when we eschew mental categories entirely, thus leaving ourselves bereft of the ability to communicate our enraptured moods.

To find this mean, quicksilvery and quivering (not solid or golden), to break our addictions to abstractions without abandoning them, to abide life's awesome upheavals without being rendered silent, we must surprise ourselves: short-circuit our generalizations, expose ourselves to irreducible "thisness," create new abstractions, express the amorphous concreteness.

If we are biology professors, we might bring a sonnet to lab; if English is our field, we could put dead frogs on our students' desks. Experiences, actual, immediate, unfamiliar, would quickly occur, and for a time, however brief, we and our students would be alive, not hovering in concepts. Abstractions would of course soon return, but these mental categories might be totally new or renewed versions of the old and might impel us to question other ratios in favor of our genius, to revise our pasts in light of eruptions of the present, to rewrite our book of life, knowing that the fresh text, too, will need to be reimagined, and that this most recent redoing will need alteration as well, and so on, until the brain runs down.

Abstractions, properly used, are fingers pointing to the moon. Without them we might never know where to look for the inexorably rounding light, but when we actually find ourselves witnessing lunar glory, we should set them quietly aside.

———

Commemorate and negate. Elevate to erase. This double vision is essential for revisionary irony. I embrace the past that has structured my habits of perception but at the same time know that this past hinders my present experience. I celebrate the present that energizes me with radically individual particulars; however, I understand that this present vitality is dependent upon traditions that have taught me the value of opening to the concrete in the first place. Saying yes and no to the same thing, hovering between authorization and invalidation, I undergo the joy of expansion, holding to opposing views at once, and the tension of contradiction, being pulled in two directions simultaneously.

This kind of irony, irreducibly duplicitous, is transcendental. No matter what my position, I know its opposite is equally valid, and so I am constantly pushed beyond wherever I stand to a counter perspective, from affirmation to cancellation. The antinomy begets a third term: a concept or image that places both sides into a productive conversation in which the interlocutors relate to one another in new and unpredictable ways, uncovering fresh virtues and unforeseen limitations. The discourse never stops, because the emerging powers and prohibitions create their own polarities that breed further talks that in turn make for additional interactions, and so on.

This is transcendence: the surpassing of one prospect for a more capacious one, the leap from the narrow known to the unknown's amplitude, from actual to possible, semantics to sublime. We think here of the fecund irony of what is known as the hermeneutical circle. When we ask a profound question, such as about the nature of creativity, we make the inquiry based on the past that has defined us. The question opens us to new information unaccounted for by the past, and so we revise our view. We can't rest, though, in this new knowledge, for we understand that it is limited by the presuppositions we bring to the question. And so we ask again about creativity, with our discoveries dictating how we put the inquiry. This asking, like the prior one, uncovers more recent knowing that challenges the just-constructed assumptions and encourages yet another query. If we are passionate in our questing, we continue this unending progression, in which each new idea grows out of all the past notions that it goes beyond and nourishes yet newer theories by which it will be eclipsed.

Transcendental ironists, we turn our lives to texts—poems, novels, essays—that endlessly revise themselves, constantly reflecting on how what has been has informed what is and on how what is will compose what will be. These loops are ceaseless: we circle back to go forward, forward to go back, each time gathering more information, becoming wider and deeper in our knowing, pushing from familiar to unfamiliar, security to risk. This is a writing that is infinite, an eternal composition, draft after draft after draft, an editorial mysticism whose goal is not the "final," but the "farther."

This incessant revision resembles the method detailed by Adrienne Rich in her feminist manifesto, "When We Dead Awaken: Writing as Re-Vision." Like Blake, she is concerned over how past texts oppress the present, especially when most of the books purvey a patriarchal ideology. While she might question Blake's nineteenth-century gender politics, radical and sensitive to women though they were, Rich would certainly approve of his way of emancipating himself from the traditions that determined him.

Here's Rich extolling ironic reading: "Re-vision—the act of looking back, of seeing with fresh eyes, of entering an old text from a new critical direction—is for women more than a chapter in cultural history: it is an act of survival." For Rich, we can only free ourselves from the past when we fully grasp its power: "Until we can understand the assumptions in which we are drenched we cannot know ourselves. . . . A radical critique of literature, feminist in its impulse, would take the work first of all as a clue to . . . how our language has trapped as well as liberated us, how the very act of naming has been till now a male prerogative, and how we can begin to see and name—and therefore live—afresh."

The conclusion: "We need to know the writing of the past, and know it differently than we have ever known it; not to pass on a tradition but to break its hold over us." And the corollary: each breaking of the past constitutes a new tradition, perhaps equally stifling, that must itself be shattered if we are to thrive.

In another context, Harold Bloom concludes much the same. Versed in Blake, Bloom grounded his theory of literary influence on the idea that imagination, properly deployed, is an act of revision. In *Anxiety of Influence*, he argues that aspiring poets acutely feel the pressure of great past writers—mainly Shakespeare and Milton—and fear that these geniuses have basically said and done it all. There's nothing new to add. So in order to create a space in which to create, a present poet must imaginatively misread past poets, showing how the writers that influenced him were limited and how his art is not.

While we need not say that Blake and other poets misread the past poets—that they engage in "misprision," to use Bloom's term—we can realize the value of imaginative perusal, of relating to texts in highly personal ways and interpreting them not in the name of objectivity but in the fulfillment of creative desire. Reading this way, we turn our imaginations into alembics through which the dull, adamantine past is broken up and reconstituted as something enduringly alive.

Blake's most obvious mode of revision is allusion. Just as Jesus related to the Jewish traditions from which he came—he annihilates what he found limiting and preserves what he can expand—so Blake associates with the canons that formed his mind. His foremost influences were the Bible, of course, and Milton's *Paradise Lost*. In his poetry, Blake persistently alludes to the Bible in such a way that he destroys its dogmatic elements—its rituals and laws—while perpetuating its prophetic energies. He rewrites Milton in a similar way. Milton was to Blake a valuable influence because he was an artist against tyranny, but he was a constraint, too, in that he valued reason over desire. In his poem focused on the seventeenth-century poet, Blake applauds the emancipating bard and abolishes, with his furious exultations, the Puritan.

But Blake revised in other, more subtle ways as well, ways that are perhaps all the more powerful for their covertness. They undo our ratios before we have time to think, burning away in a wild instant our stale layers of thought and leaving us naked near the still rising flames.

In the 1780s, when Blake was starting his career as an engraver, he wanted to illustrate the books of others — such as *The Grave* by John Blair — but he also desired to print his own creations, works in which word and image mutually illuminate each other, sometimes simply for illustrative purposes (pictures making visible the verse, poetry commenting on the image), and other times to express complicated ironies (with the image satirizing the verse, or the poem challenging the picture).

(An example of the former: the title page of *The Book of Thel*, a poem about a young virgin who fears initiation into sex and death, depicts the shepherdess standing to the side of the page and looking at a nude man grasping a woman in the picture's center. An instance of the latter appears at the end of *Thel*: the linguistic portion of the text terminates with a description of the virgin fleeing in terror from the tragedies but also the joys of the fallen world; the image following the conclusion, however, shows naked infants playfully riding a large phallic serpent. Thel, it seems, really had nothing to fear, for experience leads to true innocence, innocence as wisdom and not ignorance.)

Blake's works were often too strange to attract established publishers so he needed to come up with a method of his own for disseminating his creations. Finding that the traditional mode of printing, the letterpress, was too expensive for him to use, he tried to come up with a way that would allow him to print his art cheaply, with the tools of his own workshop. This technique came to him in a vision. Blake's brother Robert, recently deceased, appeared as a spirit and taught a special kind of relief etching. Immediately, Blake dispatched Catherine to purchase, with their last bit of money, the necessary materials.

Though not unprecedented in the history of engraving, this sort of etching was certainly not commonplace. The more popular mode involved the artist carving his designs into metal; the relief technique, in contrast, required that he *raise* the lineaments of his visions. Blake soon mastered this relief style, but added his own touch. While earlier crafts-men employed the relief method to engrave black-and-white images to illustrate words printed by the letterpress, Blake discovered a way to combine picture *and* letter in his designs, and he put color to his pages.

Blake used a hammer and chisel to cut a plate from a sheet of copper. After sketching his design onto the metal with chalk, he took a brush of camel hair, dipped it into a mixture of candle grease and salad oil, and painted onto the faint outline his poems and pictures. He had to fash-ion his forms backwards, so that they would appear in the correct direction when printed on the paper. Once his brushstrokes dried, Blake spread onto the plate a corro-sive solution called *aqua fortis*, which dissolved the parts of the copper not covered with the grease and oil. After two hours, Blake's shapes rose from the metal, about one-tenth of a millimeter. He then inked the plate with burnt oil and pressed it gently onto the paper. Once the design was set, Blake painted. Each fresh coloring was slightly different from the rest. No one version of his illuminated books is exactly like any other.

Blake refers to his printing technique in *The Marriage of Heaven and Hell*. After a devil states that the world will ap-pear infinite only through "sensual enjoyment," he asserts that this apocalypse cannot come to pass until the "notion that man has a body distinct from his soul is . . . expunged." The devil then proclaims that he will negate this erroneous dualism "by printing in the infernal method, by corrosives, which in Hell are salutary and medicinal, melting apparent surfaces away, and displaying the infinite which was hid." This process cleanses the "doors of perception."

The infernal method is a way of seeing and of saying. It is revisionary irony intensified, a retrospective gaze fervid for annihilation, dedicated to setting ablaze entire ratios — leaving behind only faint ashen phantoms — and at the same time flaming open portals to pure imaginative possibilities, clear and wide spaces where just-born forms can revel in their first experimental breathings.

Look at Blake's lines, all from *Milton*, and try to fit them into pre-existing interpretive categories. When you can't, let your mind roam among the abysmal weirdness, picturing new figures.

"Loud sounds the Hammer of Los, loud turn the Wheels of Enitharmon: / Her Looms vibrate with soft affections, weaving the Web of Life / Out from the ashes of the Dead." Who is Los? Who is Enitharmon? And what are her looms that their woofs and warps vibrate with love and resurrection?

Here is another passage that defies conception. "The Divine hand found the Two Limits: first of Opacity, then of Contraction, / Opacity was named Satan, Contraction was named Adam." What does the divine have to do with these limits? How do opacity and contraction function? Where are they? Why are they associated with Satan and Adam?

Infinity is defined: "The nature of infinity is this: That every thing has its / Own Vortex; and when once a traveller thro' Eternity / Has passed that Vortex, he perceives it roll backward behind." Is the vortex simply a perpetually churning cyclone? Is it the structure of perception, the triangular pattern made when the two eyes focus on an object? If so, is apprehension of the infinite a penetration and a passing through?

Blake disarms and even mocks our faculties for abstraction not only through his uncanny ideas. He also gives our conceptions pause through his extreme concreteness. For instance: "There is a Moment in each Day that Satan cannot find." And: "To touch each other & recede: to cross & change & return." And once more: "The Wild Thyme is Los's Messenger to Eden."

None of the quoted passages are meaningless babble; they all come to the verge of significance but veer away. The lines are indeed partly recognizable. They intimate customary figures — the demiurge, or the fall of man, or the passing from time to eternity — and they hint at ephemeral occurrences — the pulsation before the monumental conversion; motions, subtle, of loving interchange; an herb in the sun, sacred like never before. But the words don't quite cohere into clarity. They require a hermeneutical lexicon that has been lost. Blake was true to a confession he once made: "That which can be made Explicit to the Idiot is not worth my care."

Blake's compositions corrode the encrusted abstractions and generate radically individual systems resistant — and this is a paradox — to systemization. His ideas and images almost unmoor from meaning. To make his language significant, we must forge new mental connections, must relate the strange verbal units to our individual histories. These relationships give the bizarre line original significations while also charging the personal experience with fresh energy.

This prolific conversation between text and reader, in which each newly defines the other, is not a self-contained occurrence but only one instant in an endless interpretive dialogue. Regardless of the rigor of the analysis, Blake's terms remain irreducible to conclusive readings. His poems invite infinite hermeneutics. If we accept the invitation, then each time we encounter his poems we imagine unexplored terrains, for ourselves and the words.

Literary critic Jerome McGann captures the impetus behind Blake's poetry: "What was needed was an art that could not be turned into an abstraction, an art that no one would fall down and worship. It must be an art that would urge no programs and offer no systems. He [Blake] found it in an art which was ultimately committed not to creation but, paradoxically, to destruction, an art that would not be seen but would be seen through." What Walter Benjamin said of Kafka is true of Blake: both writers "took precautions against the interpretation of [their] writing."

Blake's creations do what Shelley thinks all great poetry should do: strip away "the veil of familiarity from the world" and lay "bare the naked and sleeping beauty, which is the spirit of its forms." To read Blake well is to expand with his outlandishness, to amplify his curious tropes and figures as Blake would enlarge a sand's grain: with an ever-turning spiral of perspectives, now widening, now narrowing, or both at once. If you're going to get the spirit of Blake, you have to be, in your own way, Blake. If you're going to grasp his poetry, you have to be a poet.

The works of Blake are "writerly," to use Roland Barthes' term. Opposed to "readerly" books that reinforce, in untroubled language, a culture's conventions, "writerly" texts upset commonsensical expectations through sentences resistant to institutionalization. Reading a "writerly" work, we must actively transform ultimately inaccessible elements into temporarily meaningful patterns. We become "no longer a consumer but a producer of the text." We find ourselves actually writing our own works, enjoying the "infinite play of the world" before it is "traversed, intersected, stopped, plasticized by some singular system (Ideology, Genus, Criticism) which reduces the plurality of entrances, the opening of networks, the infinity of languages."

Emerson once wrote the following: "There is then creative reading as well as creative writing." Near the end of his "Song of Myself," Walt Whitman asserts that "I am the teacher of athletes, / He that by me spreads a wider breast than my own proves the width of my own, / He most honors my style who learns under it to destroy the teacher." This is the role of the teacher: not to stifle students with overweening authority but to free them into creations that might surpass his own.

In his preface to *Jerusalem*, Blake wrote what poet Alicia Ostriker calls the "first free-verse manifesto in English." He complains of the constraints of regular rhythm, the "Monotonous Cadence, like that used by Milton and Shakespeare and all writers of English Blank Verse." He further chafes against the "bondage of Rhyming." To escape these "awkward" conventions, Blake employs more flexible forms: "variety in every line, both of cadences & number of syllables." But his irregular rhythms are not random. "Every word & every letter," he says, "is studied and put into its fit place: the terrific numbers are reserved for the terrific parts—the mild & gentle for the mild & gentle parts, and the prosaic, for inferior parts: all are necessary to each other." These poetic experimentations are more than aesthetic choices; they are definitive for the entire culture. "Poetry Fetter'd," Blake asserts, "Fetters the Human Race!"

Blake's content is unrelentingly intractable. His form is as well. He is probably the first poet in English to see form not as prior to content but as an extension of content. The shifting mood and tone of the poem, not a commitment to blank verse or heroic couplets, dictate rhythm and meter. This organic unfolding of form—which influenced the later prosodic innovations of Charles Olson and Robert Creeley—inspired in Blake highly original stylistic innovations.

Not surprisingly, given his manifesto, he often wrote in free verse, as these lines from *Jerusalem* show:

> The Vegetative Universe opens like a flower from the
>   Earth's center,
> In which is Eternity. It expands in Stars to the Mundane
>   Shell

And there it meets Eternity again, both within and
    without,
And the abstract Voids between the Stars are the
    Satanic Wheels.

He was also one of the inaugural prose poets. In *The Marriage of Heaven and Hell*, he opens with a conventional lyric but then expresses his ideas in unmetered, unbroken sentences: "Without Contraries is no progression. Attraction and Repulsion, Reason and Energy, Love and Hate, are necessary to Human existence. From these contraries spring what the religious call Good & Evil. Good is the passive that obeys Reason. Evil is the active springing from Energy. Good is Heaven. Evil is Hell."

Additionally, Blake experimented with nonlinear form. Traditional narrative structures simply couldn't accommodate his manifold visions, in which single events are presented from numerous simultaneous perspectives. In *Milton*, for instance, the descent of the seventeenth-century poet to earth from the deadening heaven of his own imagining is detailed in several shifting panels of verse, each of which offers a distinct reaction to the event.

Moreover, Blake's commitment to energy over form encouraged him to transcend generic categories. Some of his works mix poetry and prose, prophecy and satire. Others meld epic and tragedy. Still others are simultaneously children's songs and penetrating dramatic monologues.

Blake created beyond all definition; it is reductive even to call him a poet or a painter, since his works also qualify as theology, philosophy, psychology, and history. In fact, it doesn't make entire sense to call him an iconoclast, since at times he seemed untouched by the traditions that shaped him, as though he didn't need to worry about breaking icons he had already transcended.

As we know, of course, Blake was acutely aware of the impossibility of creating in a vacuum, free of influence. Still, what perhaps distinguished Blake from most any poet before or after was his extreme individuality, unparalleled and inimitable — even if his inventiveness was, by necessity, not sui generis. Blake remains an exemplar of uncompromising artistic integrity. He courageously held to his visions even though he was ridiculed and ignored. His hope was that his outré and empyreal poetics would one day find an audience worthy of the enigmatic revelation. His wish has by now undoubtedly been fulfilled, but long after the termination of his sublunar course.

In *Milton*, Blake describes three classes of men: the elect, the reprobate, and the redeemed. The elect, exemplified by Satan, believe that the universe is static, a system of laws that fully determine what a creature can be. This is the cosmos of Newton, quite amenable, it turns out, to the hardcore Calvinist's conviction that souls are predestined to be condemned or saved. Blake suggests that this deadening worldview is prevalent in his time, bolstering the tyrannical king who wants complacent subjects and supporting the orthodox clergyman desirous of sanctioning his blessedness.

There is no place for the artist in this satanic domain. The secular and religious rulers fear the power of art to inspire the populace to question the status quo, imagine a democracy, and create forms conducive to equality. And so king and priest demonize the poets, exile them to the outskirts, call them reprobate. The poet thus becomes the prophet crying in the wilderness, the madman preaching in the alley, the avant-garde's monstrous forerunner, the bête noir, the criminal, the prince of the underground, the spawn of Cain, the scapegoat. Ignored or ridiculed or, worse, in danger of incarceration in a prison or an asylum, the reprobate poet — whom Blake calls Rintrah — requires tremendous courage to hold his vision. What bolsters him most is the hope that one day his art will inspire a sympathetic audience to destroy the oppressive system that ousted him and build a more charitable metropolis in its place. Then he will no longer be the reprobate but the redeemed.

The redeemed poet, figured in *Milton* as Palamabron, works within society, not from without. He moves in the precincts of the tyrant, acknowledging that the world is fallen — botched, ignorant, duplicitous, tragic, evil — and that he himself is as well. Accordingly, he makes the melancholy fields of experience the places of his labor. His vocation is to transform the lapsed imaginations of his culture into capable creative faculties, to awaken in everyone the artist, the Christ within, to turn the wilds into an exquisite city of jewels. He strives to do this by delving into his most personal sensibilities and expressing them in language close to his idiosyncrasy. Doing so, he exemplifies the true path to art and encourages his audience to take the same direction. If they do, the result will be sublime. In living a life true to their individual imaginations, they will all eventually find concord one with the other, becoming integral players in a communal effort to construct the New Jerusalem.

To turn from reprobate to redeemed: this was Blake's own fantasy, and it might be ours as well. To follow Blake's example, in life and art, is to become peculiar. Express your thoughts and feelings, however bizarre, in language appropriate to their aberrance, even if the sentences make sense only to you. Maybe no one will pay any attention or maybe you'll be mocked. But in the end, if you stay close to strangeness, and if you represent it with some accuracy, then eventually your utterances will draw an audience. The more deeply you descend into your specific haunts, the more universal you become.

Writing is rewriting, and vision, revision. What we call first drafts might emerge from immediate inspiration—the world in the grain of sand or the egret stalking through mud or a sudden swish of unnamed green. Writers hunger for moments like these—they are so rare. When these instants occur, eruptions of not-yet-conceptualized exuberance, then the writer wants to represent in language the force of the perception. And so words pour out—forceful verbs and florid adjectives and adverbs that are fulsome, long sinewy sentences, paragraphs sloppy and jumbled, punctuation wide apart, little buoys in a tumultuous ocean of loquacity. But other times, the encounter is not ecstatic but diaphanous, too fleeting and vague for turbid verbiage, and the terms are terse, with etched syntax and denuded nouns— quiet gestures toward wisps just gone.

Each linguistic extreme, already a revision of the ungraspable moment, a reduction of thing to thought, is nebulous, either too near to the vision's intensity or too distant. The problem is one Wallace Stevens well knew: we need to know where to stand to behold the sublime. When we find this place, we are in the moment's grip but also beyond it, transforming our enthrallment into symbols that will consume our readers as we are right now absorbed.

Zen poet Bashō once said, "How admirable, to see lightning, and not think life is fleeting." Sensing the flash unaided by allegory—this is the shock of the real. But Bashō, to say this in a haiku, had to look back to the faded fire and fit it into a traditional structure, an old binary—to allegorize or not to allegorize.

The gap between event and art, occurrence and opinion, is successful revision's region, where the writer finds the apt area between what happened and what she wants to depict. So many redrafts fail, clingy or aloof, overly mushy or too clipped. This is why revision must be almost endless, and difficult—proper calibration is almost impossible to achieve. But this is also the joy of amending—each new alteration might find that shred of space where the numinous and the naming meet and perfectly merge, where the language is vibrant without being turgid, lucid without being stiff, where sentences whip and snap in the still strong currents of their inspiration but the flag holds, a beacon bright and sturdy.

As we know, every time Blake printed his words and images, no matter how enthusiastic his imagination, he was revising, necessarily, and frequently with astounding success. The final step of his printing process, his coloring of the design, ensured that each copy of a particular sheet, as well as every copy of the book, would be different from the others, however slightly. Though Blake might have used the same hues and proportions for a specific printed design, a small change in his brushstroke, maybe intentional, maybe not, or a minor shift in mood or desire, made each version distinct, a freestanding work of art.

Blake's title page for *The Marriage of Heaven and Hell* features an image of enclasped lovers rising from burning billows. The leaf exists in several copies. Each is unique. The color tone in the so-called Fitzwilliam copy, for instance, is much darker and denser than the one in the Morgan Library and Museum copy. Was Blake fresher, more energetic, maybe angrier, when he painted the former? Was he more tranquil and gentle when he put brush to the latter?

We can't know the answer to these questions, but we can understand that each of Blake's pages was a *revision* of his earlier intention, an intention expressed by the permanent designs on the engraved plates, and also by his prior paintings of the printed lineaments. Any particular painted page—no matter now spontaneous or inspired, however deliberate or plodding—constituted something new, unrepeatable, and maybe at that moment, in Blake's mind, perfect. But the next coloring of the sheet differed from the earlier creation, and also generated a novel, idiosyncratic picture, perhaps exactly the one to which Blake, in that instant, aspired. But the next painted copy changed the picture yet again, and so on, until Blake printed as many books as he wanted. Even then, however, the revising didn't stop, for Blake had before him several copies, any one of which at any given time might appear to fulfill his ideal. Each image, regardless of when it was made, revised the others, incessantly.

The plates themselves, of course, were revisions of his artistic ideas which in turn were reviews of his immediate visions — themselves, at the moment he articulated them in his mind, revisions of sublime experiences beyond representation. No drafts, no matter how proximate to the inspiration, are first drafts. The best one can produce is a second draft, and that draft is probably already a third or fourth. There's no such thing as writing that is not revision.

This is liberating for those of us who fixate on the alleged brilliance of what we call our first drafts, either because we think these early efforts retain the potency of the inspiration or because we trust in spontaneity. The young draft, though, no matter how promising it might be, is almost never our best writing. To be freed from the notion that first drafts even exist, to understand that you're already revising the minute you put word to page: this makes it easier to modify those initial sentences. There's nothing special about them. They're yesterday's news.

The importance of revision is obvious. Almost every writing handbook emphasizes repeated editing. The most famous ones certainly do: John Gardner's *On Becoming a Novelist*, Ursula K. Le Guin's *Steering the Craft*, and Jacques Barzun's *Simple & Direct*. "There are always too many words at first," Barzun says. Le Guin agrees: "Forced to weigh your words, you find out which are the styrofoam and which are the heavy gold. Severe cutting intensifies your style." In the words of Gardner: "Fiction does not spring into the world full grown, like Athena. It is the process of writing and re-writing that makes fiction original and profound."

Almost any other writer would encourage the same. (But maybe all we need is Hemingway: "First drafts are shit.") What Blake's idea of creation does is make it easier for us to revise. We are never not revising, so we can't avoid what we're already doing, and thus we might as well make the best of it, or perhaps do more: realize that revising is creating, is life, and therefore the more beautiful our revisions, the more vital our lives, and, surprisingly, the more innocent.

A friend of Blake's, Thomas Butts, once paid the poet a visit. After knocking on the door and receiving no answer, Butts let himself in. He found the dwelling empty, and so made his way to the garden in back. He knew that William and Catherine often spent time there. Entering, he heard Blake call from a summer house at the plot's end. "Come in," the poet said. "It's only Adam and Eve, you know." When Butts reached the house, he saw man and wife within, stark naked, reading passages from *Paradise Lost*.

This little story is worth telling solely for its charm but it also points to one of Blake's obsessions: innocence. For Blake, innocence is a way of seeing as much as a state of being. To witness the world innocently is to perceive it not as something fixed and static but as a shifting, flexible, subtle field of energy, forever fresh and fascinating, and always inspiring strong emotions. When we are innocent, we approach the imaginative state, the felicities of vision, for our hearts are kindly disposed — not selfishly pinched or detached, uncaring. Nature appears not as separate and threatening, an object that exists "out there" only to thwart our human fantasies; nature arises rather as an interface of human and nonhuman, where the human desire for the infinite merges with unlimited possibility, where love of the world finds reciprocation. Innocence, then, is not naiveté. It is knowledge: "Unorganized Innocence, An Impossibility / Innocence dwells with Wisdom but never with Ignorance."

Blake believed that innocence was indispensable for his art. He was especially concerned with innocence early in his career, when he published *Songs of Innocence*. His vision of innocence in this collection is complex. Even though the enchanting lyrics present a frolicking pastoral landscape, there are somber forces lurking among the lambs and the children and the lilies. The inaugural verse in the book explores this mixture of blitheness and solemnity.

The poem, called "Introduction," opens with a shepherd piping songs in wild valleys. He sees a giggling child who floats on a cloud. The child directs the shepherd to play a song about a lamb, and when he does so, the child weeps with joy. The cloudy figure then tells the shepherd to forgo his pipe and sing the song, and once more the shepherd obliges, and again the child happily cries. Next the child commands the shepherd to write down his song in a book "that all may read." He vanishes as the shepherd carries out the order:

> And I plucked a hollow reed,
>
> And I made a rural pen,
> And I stain'd the water clear,
> And I wrote my happy songs
> Every child may joy to hear.

This first song of innocence is actually, and surprisingly, about a fall: from unity with nature to division (the shepherd violates his environment by plucking the reed); from proximity to a supernatural child to distance from it (the child disappears as the shepherd makes ready to write); from immediate artistic expression to mediated (instrumental music, nonconceptual, devolves into writing, dependent upon gaps between words and ideas); and from clear audience response to ambiguous (the first two songs clearly inspire the child to weep with joy while the written version *might* cause children to experience joy).

Innocence requires experience to escape ignorance. The way most see innocence — as a state preceding knowledge of opposites, such as good and evil — flattens the condition to a one-sided perspective. Blake's innocence, though, is a wide knowing that accommodates antinomies, like simplicity and complexity, unity and diversity, and even itself and its opposite, experience. We can only know innocence when we have lost it (just as we can only know wholeness through wound, and concord by way of confusion). The lack of innocence teaches us its power to relieve us from the pains of experience: evil with no good in sight, bewildering duplicity, imprisonment in a consistent identity. In innocence's absence, its fullness arrives.

If experience is actuality, in which you are *this* person and little else (this husband, father, and writer, with dwindling options for change), then innocence is exhilarating potentiality, where you might become anything you want, creating roles that suit your fancy. If experience is constrained to the past (you look backward with nostalgia or regret) and locked into a future (to which you look forward with anticipation or fear), then innocence lives closest to the present, electric and antic. Where experience is paralyzed by self-consciousness (the cloying shame produced by seeing oneself through the critical eyes of others), innocence is unaware of the gazes of other people; it is spontaneous, unaffected. Experience approximates ratio, narcissistic transformation of events into selfish prejudices; innocence, as has been suggested, nears poetic genius, the imaginative life, the convivial attitude toward sublimities beyond the self.

Innocence births creativity. It is a return, from the point of view of experience, to a mental space where playful possibilities hold sway, where it's always surprise day—anything might happen. In this state, life is indeed for a brief time a meandering cloud from which creatures inspire us to make unprecedented songs. Of course we soon separate ourselves from this exciting responsiveness—what Wordsworth called a "spontaneous overflow of powerful feeling"—in order to reflect upon it, to write it down, to recollect the "emotion" in "tranquility." But for a small period we are young again, and dreaming about what we might be when we grow up.

Immanuel Kant compared the aesthetic to play. When we are in an artistic mood we don't connect life to scientific laws or moral principles but rather in a disinterested fashion let the mind go where it will. Kant called this disposition "purposiveness without a purpose." His disciple Friedrich Schiller agreed, likening the composition and the appreciation of art to a condition in which we are freed from our two limiting drives, toward nature's flux and toward abstract form, and able to play with the virtues of both without suffering the vices of either. Friedrich Schelling translated these ideas into his notion of freedom; he argued that unpredictable play, in the guise of chaos, is the origin of liberty, of human choice and thus imagination and morality.

Blake's *Songs of Innocence* are full of children playing and laughing. The shepherd, in the introduction, plays his songs. In "The Echoing Green," old folks enjoy watching the children at their games. The entire forest gambols in "Laughing Song."

Nietzsche said that he knew of "no other way of associating with *great tasks* than *play*." He also thought that a man can only become mature after he has "rediscovered the seriousness he had as a child at play." For him, as for Blake, play is essential to knocking over the old hoary idols and dreaming up new ones in their place and experimenting with the quick forms that might bring these reveries to life.

For the artist, play is the path to wizened mastery. The maker must return to emotional and mental turbulence. She must let the abysmal unconscious bubble up. She must unmoor her cables, cut her anchors. In the sudden unknown, she might think she's in the void. But if she endures the disorientation, she'll realize that this nothingness is plenitude, a huge reservoir of unrealized potential. There she discovers her angels and her demons, and casts into the undulating waters.

Casts are flings into the waves. Casts are also structures for fluids, molds in which liquid hardens. Both kinds of casting are required for art, for full realization of poetic genius: a conversation between vision and ratio. The potencies of innocence must be actualized if they are to be revealed — chaos requires order; play, rules. "Energy" might be the "only life," as Blake claims in *The Marriage of Heaven and Hell*, but this bodily force finds expression only in the "Reason," "the bound or outward circumference of Energy."

Such is Blake's *felix culpa*, happy fall: just as one can only find regeneration by falling into generation (redemption through sinning; union through fracture), so the artist can discover the extent of his capabilities only by reflecting on them, from a distance, and then finding for them an aesthetic pattern.

Blake examines experience in *Songs of Experience*. While *Songs of Innocence* features a pastoral world, *Songs of Experience* exhibits a more challenging geography, often urban, where children and adults alike suffer injustice, sadness, fear, cruelty. But as was the case with innocence, Blake's idea of experience is not one-dimensional. Without experience, there is no innocence, so if innocence is a desirable state — and it is — surely the postlapsarian state possesses virtue.

The introduction to *Songs of Experience* begins authoritatively. The voice of a Bard, who "present, past, and future, sees," commands the audience to heed his words. Not only does he grasp all dimensions of time, he also has "heard / The Holy Word / That walked among the ancient tree." Either the Bard himself or the Word that he comprehends — the duplicitous syntax suggests both options — calls the "lapsed soul" of the earth. This fallen soul, we understand, "might control / The starry pole, / And fallen, fallen light renew!"

Given this possibility, the Bard — or the Word with which he is associated — beseeches the declining world to rise up from its gloomy torpor and reclaim its vivacious beauty.

The Bard is the shepherd poet grown-up. He now no longer enjoys a childish muse who drifts on a cloud and inspires blithe songs. Instead he is immured in tragic time, which destroys everything, and he laments this dark temporality, weeping over the earth's fallen souls and their perverse decision not to ascend.

But the hardened poet has strengths that the pasture's lyricist lacks. He possesses a broad knowledge of history's complexities, of how the mysterious past shapes the perplexing present, and this present informs the future, nerve-wracking. We are finite, born to die, and only with this understanding can we learn of renewed life, eternity. The Bard also comprehends the "Holy Word," the logos, which spoke the universe into existence — "Let there be light" — and which incarnates the divine — serving, in the Gospel of John, as the abiding beam that "shines in the darkness." The Bard has suffered the creative word's absence, undergone the painful fractures of the fallen world: between human and nature, human and human, human and God, and, perhaps worst of all, between ego and self-consciousness, the shameful state in which one always suspects that another set of eyes is watching him, judging him, intending him harm. Aware of these lacerations, the Bard understands the Word's harmonizing light, its ubiquitous elixirs. He recognizes, like Dickinson, that "Water, is taught by thirst."

The next poem of Songs of Experience, "Earth's Answer," describes the earth's response to the Bard's plea. She doesn't understand his invitation for rebirth, mistaking his generous voice for that of a tyrannical heavenly father who shackles erotic energy. Such is the fallen world — miscommunication reigns, as do blindness, jealousy, and terror.

But, as the Bard's presence intimates, there are, amidst the pernicious things, vigorous forces and penetrating insights inaccessible to the innocent. Think of Blake's famous lyric, "The Tyger," in which the beast, though pictured as a horrifying product of a demonic god, burns brightly in the dark forests, leaving men and women breathless over its "fearful symmetry." Or recall "The Chimney Sweeper." In the piece, the speaker demonstrates a profound perspicacity of the psychology of envy, claiming that his parents forced him to clean chimneys in the city—a grim, deadly job—*because* he was "happy upon the heath." His guardians coveted his happiness. When they concluded that they would never enjoy it, they decided to take it away from their son, reasoning: if we can't have it, then no one can.

Another potent boon of the fall is erotic energy, the fire in the loins that often results—as Ginsberg discovered in the Harlem apartment—in spiritual vision and artistic creativity. In *The Book of Thel*, Blake, as I noted earlier, explores the dangers of being overly committed to virginity, a state not yet agitated by sexual reproduction and thus by an awareness of the great cycles of growth and decay, life and death. Thel the young maiden dwelling in the Eden-like Vales of Har fears the two most powerful elements of the fallen world—sex and death. Her cowardice before these difficult yet necessary forces results in stasis. At the poem's end, the earth generously offers Thel an encounter with the terrors but also the pleasures of experience: the joys of charity, of helping those who suffer, and the ecstasies of the senses, "honey from every wind." The girl recoils from these possibilities, however, and rushes back to her enclosed habitat. Though there she will certainly be safe from the frustrations of the fall, such as aggression and repression, she will also be excluded from the enduring delights found only to Eden's east: bountiful grace and bodily desire fulfilled.

In 1793, four years after *Thel*, Blake in *Visions of the Daughters of Albion* details the delights of sexual experience. Oothon, the poem's main female character, is the exact opposite of Thel: where the maiden of Har refuses fullness, Oothon embraces it. She is glad for "happy copulation," especially for the exhilarating "moment of desire" in which the woman "shall awaken her womb to enormous joys / In the secret shadows of her chamber." Unfortunately, Oothon's espousal of "happy happy Love," "free as the mountain wind," exposes her to danger. One male character, Bromion, takes her erotic openness as an invitation to rape her and then to revile her as a wanton who deserved what she got; another, her lover Theotormon, rejects her as impure after the violation, viewing her sexuality as a mark of unforgivable sin.

Such are the dangers of the lapsed world, where orgasmic thrills are frequently inseparable from violent reprisals. Regardless, Blake reveled in sex. In his notebooks, he drew numerous erotic images, some surreal (a nude woman with a cathedral for a vagina), but most centered on the erect phallus. He drafted, for instance, a woman reaching toward a man's large penis while apparently masturbating, and a boy in an aroused state watching a couple copulate. Most notably, in his original self-portrait for *Milton*, Blake is nude with an erect penis that is for some reason blackened. (Later editors, prudish, covered this image with knickers.)

His lustiness apparently went well beyond mere drawing, though, and it at times troubled his otherwise harmonious marriage. Alexander Gilchrist, Blake's first biographer, claimed that Blake's union with Catherine was threatened in the early years with "not wholly unprovoked" jealousy. Gilchrist never mentioned the cause of the jealous feelings, but Swinburne did. In his essay on the poet, he claimed that Blake once, while in a "patriarchal mood," proposed that he add a second wife to his household. Mrs. Blake tearfully objected and the plan was soon dropped.

"Embraces are Cominglings: from the Head even to the Feet." "The lust of the goat is the bounty of God." Men and

women most "require / The lineaments of Gratified Desire."
These lines, coupled with Blake's designs on a concubine,
suggest that the man was simply libidinous, and that's all.
He was certainly that, but he also saw his concupiscence as
an integral part of the creative process, holding that the fire
of desire can generate artistic effusions: "He whose Gates
are open'd in those Regions of the Body / Can from those
Gates view all these wondrous Imaginations." No dualist,
Blake indeed believed that sensual fulfillment and mental production complement one another: "Enjoyment &
not Abstinence is the food of Intellect." In fact, for Blake,
the erotic energies frequently excoriated by the religiously
orthodox are inseparable from the soul's most resplendent
moments: "What are called vices in the natural world, are
the highest sublimities in the spiritual world."

Blake's mingling of the spirit and the body was by no
means uncommon in late eighteenth- and early nineteenth-
century London. As Marsha Schuchard has shown, the poet
came of age in a countercultural milieu, composed mainly
of Moravians and Swedenborgians, in which sexuality and
religion were thoroughly interdependent: the hormones get
you to heaven, and paradise is within the genitalia. Long
maintained in the Tantric traditions of India and the Taoist
ones of China, this holy eroticism thrived in the works of
Count Zinzendorf, the great Moravian theologian, and
Emanuel Swedenborg, the Swedish visionary, both of whom
spent time in London in the middle years of the eighteenth
century and whose theories influenced the radical Protes-
tantism espoused by Blake's family and Blake himself. Zinzendorf and Swedenborg alike believed that sexual virility
was spiritual power: God is energy, vitality, life, manifesting
most intensely in those stunningly intimate instances that
hum the abundance of cosmos and perennially teach us that
the only right sentiments are praise and appreciation.

Blake's central belief, possibly gleaned from these erotic
theologies of his time, but more likely from his own experi-

ence, was this: "everything that lives is holy." And nothing is more alive than sexual drive and satisfaction, more electric with unprecedented and large and marvelous feelings that inspire those epochal thoughts we never forget: everything's bigger, by far, than I thought; anything might happen on the topsy-turvy earth, like a snake might turn into a bird; I can do anything I want, make anything, from a sonnet to an astonishing mountainous altar. Certainly this jolting wonder frequently brings into being creativity, a need to express the ecstasy not only in orgasm but also in art.

Perhaps the most powerful art is indeed libido transformed, lust turned into arousing linguistic rhythms, pleasurably expanding and contracting, or images that are colorful and lush, engorged yet flowing. Freud would say so; he called this process of transmutation, sublimation, and claimed that it was essential for civilization to rise out of savagery, for the city to give elegant form to the wild. Whatever we call this almost miraculous metamorphosis — quivering flesh into sibilant iambs — we have all likely encountered its culminations, and in doing so have learned in our innermost fibers the essential value of what Thel denied and Oothon celebrated: the throbbing polarities of the organic world, those forces driving our bodies toward copulation and composition, not to mention toward dance or sport, those exquisite concords of flesh and grace.

To oppose the body or to repress its urges is to dam the spring of art. The ascetic is the hack; the genius loves abandon. The word sought the flesh. Let your carnality pursue the poem.

GENERATION

If we don't move beyond innocence, we won't experience the earth's awesome energies, sexual and otherwise, and the involved wisdom they inspire. We won't become "human," Blake's noblest state, defined by the ability not only to encounter but also actively to manipulate tense, productive oppositions, including experience and innocence as well as longing and satisfaction, imagination and ratio, vision and memory.

Blake calls the fallen world "Generation," a realm, as he writes in *Four Zoas*, where "Life lives upon Death & by devouring appetite / All things subsist on one other." But though Generation is a Darwinian struggle for survival, it is also the image of "regeneration," which is the "point of mutual forgiveness between Enemies" and the "Birthplace of the Lamb of God incomprehensible!" Mercy, the impetus for the forgiveness that reconciles enemies, can grow only among the tormenting divisions.

Generation is required for regeneration. To remain too long in the state of innocence is to descend into hell. Blake often likens innocence to "Beulah"—less a place than a psychological disposition marked by playful fancy, moony reverie, and romantic dreaming, soporific tempers in which normally constructive contraries for a time come to rest. Although it is a state of refurbishing possibility, of necessary recovery, Beulah can become something else if one languishes there longer than need be. Beulah can metamorphose into "Ulro," Blake's term for that hellish condition in which one falls into inaction, total stasis, in which oppositions disappear and with them any chance for creation. The sweet garden of Beulah, a natural paradise, enclosed and shaded, devolves into a monotonous rocky desert.

Properly used, Beulah is the muse, the restorer of artists

exhausted from creative strife. Once re-energized, these artists channel the imaginative currents required for inhabit-
ing the true paradise, the spiritual one, where the contraries
endlessly separate and battle and unite into more intense
and beautiful forms of being. This is Eden, what Blake calls
"Regeneration," "Eternity," and also the "Human"—the
artistic character, the awakening of genius, the Jesus on the
inside.

———

Now we understand a seeming contradiction in Blake's use
of "allegory" as a concept. We remember that he contrasts
allegory with vision, favoring vision as an immediate grasp
of a particular instant and devaluing allegory as ratio. Allegory connects to experience, where perceptions are ciphers
of thoughts, where a rose is valuable only as a sign of love
or a nightingale only worthy for its gestures toward poetic
melody. In contrast, vision is close to innocence, in which
one delights in stirring encounters without being overly
aware of what's going on, in which the crimson petals turn
the heart sanguine and the unseen bird illuminates the twi-
light.

In another passage, though, Blake calls allegory "sublime." He imagines that he will speak to "future generations
by a Sublime Allegory which is now perfectly completed
into a Grand Poem." This allegory will be "addressed to the
Intellectual powers while it is altogether hidden from the
Corporeal Understanding." The epic work will constitute
the "Most Sublime Poetry."

Blake might simply be, for unknown reasons, substi-
tuting allegory for vision; perhaps he changed his mind
about which word was most suitable for designating inspiration. But his confusion in terminology might actually reveal something about allegory as a mode of comprehension
and apprehension. Maybe Blake means that allegory, in the
sense that he inflected it in the other passage (the one about

how it's inferior to vision), is not entirely negative. Obviously, allegory as opposed to vision, can, like ratio, be dangerous if we believe that it is the only method for perceiving and expressing—if we think that the abstract is superior to the concrete. However, if we see allegory as the complementary opposition to vision (and analogously, generation as the required counterpart of regeneration), then allegory becomes an essential element of immediate seeing.

First of all, we can't even appreciate the significance of particular visions until we connect them to general ideas. Secondly, we can't translate minute perceptions into works of art unless we self-consciously transform these individual encounters into symbols. Finally, our very desire for vision in the first place is dependent upon allegory: we can only grasp the enduring meaning of vision through conceptualization, through the gap between event and reflection, fullness and yearning.

For Blake, poetic creation is not some otherworldly affair, a pristine process that avoids life's excruciating rifts, its gashes and blood, its unrequited desires, its tragedies and losses, its imprisoning ideologies and alienating systems. The creation of poetry is instead a matter of embracing the world as it is, sinking deep into its fury and mire, acknowledging the inevitability of tyranny perpetrated in the name of reason. Only in descending into the muck, only in entering into the cruel ideologue's debates, can the poet understand the exquisite convolutions, how the grossest clods and the most dangerous ideas can burst into prodigal beings.

In "Circus Animals' Desertion," Yeats claims that his "masterful images" might grow from his "pure mind," but these symbols began in "the foul rag and bone shop of the heart." Some days the artist can innocently play in his mind's unhindered arenas, where anything can happen, and where there is always rising something gorgeous and uncharted.

But these days, as all artists know, are so seldom. Usually the work must be unearthed from the darker heart: suffering and deprivation and bereavement and refuse. From what is most broken sometimes comes the trope most whole.

Blake's "Nervous Fear" rarely let him rest. Frequently he stumbled into "a Deep Pit of Melancholy, Melancholy without any real reason for it." He wanted so much to emancipate himself from these most wicked parts of Generation and elevate to Eden — the imagination, nimble and shimmering.

But he knew that it was precisely the devitalizing shadows that impelled him to seek the fertile light. He hung on the wall of his workshop a print of Dürer's *Melencolia*, which personifies the dejected mood as a fallen angel enclosed in a cramped cell, where useless instruments of measure are strewn all around. In the gaze of this grounded spirit, though, is noble contemplation, the ache for wisdom. As Dürer knew, melancholia, in spite of its tortures, is also a muse, a spur to meditation and imagination. It is the "wakeful anguish," as Keats says, that throws us into what we most need to live: morning roses and round peonies and the eyes, beyond compare, of those we love.

Consider the common fly. Most only notice it as a pest to be swatted or a reminder of carrion and feces. The fly is thus usually only a ratio, an allegory, for all that threatens our sense of sovereignty—death, obviously, but also all those little droning nuisances that daily bother our peace. If we are to live, though, we must demolish this abstraction and release the fly into infinity.

> Seest thou the little winged fly, smaller than a grain of
>   sand?
> It has a heart like thee; a brain open to heaven & hell,
> Withinside wondrous & expansive; its gates are not
>   clos'd:
> I hope thine are not: hence it clothes itself in rich array;
> Hence thou art cloth'd with human beauty O thou
>   mortal man.
> Seek not thy heavenly father then beyond the skies:
> There Chaos dwells & ancient Night & Og & Anak old:
> For every human heart has gates of brass & bars of
>   adamant,
> Which few dare unbar because dread Og & Anak guard
>   the gates
> Terrific! and each mortal brain is wall'd and moated
>   round
> Within: and Og & Anak watch here; here is the Seat
> Of Satan in its Webs; for in brain and heart and loins
> Gates open behind Satan's Seat to the City of
>   Golgonooza,
> Which is the spiritual fourfold London, in the loins of
>   Albion.

Freed of the ratio, the fly is an incandescent cosmos. We, too, cleansed of abstraction, enormously expand. But we shut down our corridors of vision; we lock in icy chains the unlimited grandeurs of our minds. We construct our own internal Ogs and Anaks, giants who barred the Hebrews from the Promised Land. And in so doing, we submit to Satan — not the evil imp but the habit, forged in the name of bland comfort, of stifling our own creativity, which is god-like in its scope and potency, and attributing it to a tyrannical deity in the sky. This craven failure to take up our vital powers is all the more perverse because just outside of our self-fashioned cold confinements springs the seat of art itself — Golgonooza, Blake's term for the human ability to transform the wilderness into a beautiful city where charity, generosity, and poetry preside, a metropolis fully humanized, a person (Albion) more than a series of buildings. When we activate this aptitude, we spiritualize flies and places as large as London, converting them, through our affectionate imaginations, from static stuff to dynamic gatherings of the quaternions of the universe, such as reason, emotion, sensation, and instinct; earth, air, fire, and water; spring, summer, winter, and fall.

You look at the fly, or the nautilus, or the December spruce, or the solar eye and the purplish clouds meandering in its beams, or the smallest chink of mica, and under your intense gaze it breaks through your predetermined conceptions of its meaning and bursts into something never seen before, a coruscating vortex of images and significations. It stokes your imagination into fresh creations, new relations — allegories or theories or comparisons or judgments — and these conceits solidify for a time into ratios. The fly now betokens your visionary powers and the tragedy of your not using them, and the speck of mica suggests that all the earth is a crystal, perpetually refracting white light into flourishing hues. But these ratios are only tenuous and temporary because your eye remains keen on concreteness and thus will soon once more feel the reason shattering before the ever-burgeoning sensual.

In 1800, the Blakes moved from their beloved London to Felpham, a seaside village in Sussex. They came at the invitation of William Hayley, a successful poet and biographer who admired Blake's engravings and wished to offer his patronage. Financially strapped, Blake hoped that a good relationship with Hayley would lead to consistent work. After three years on the coast, though, the Blakes were keen on returning to the city.

Blake's relationship with Hayley had turned sour. While in Felpham, Blake was aflame with visions, and he was fervidly transmuting them into art. He didn't want to be bothered with Hayley's minor engraving jobs and moreover bristled at his patron's dismissive attitude toward his blossoming poetic powers. This was a tense time for Blake, one of crisis, when he found his unconventional creations at odds with Hayley's conventional taste. Blake was anxious, nervous, often angry. These volatile emotions contributed forcefully to an incident that almost got him killed.

One hot day in August, a soldier named John Scofield appeared in the Blakes' Felpham garden. Blake saw the man loitering about the foliage. Unaware that his gardener had asked Scofield for help, Blake took the soldier for a trespasser and demanded to know his intentions. When the soldier, who was drunk, replied in a belligerent tone, Blake insisted that he leave the garden immediately. An argument ensued. Ill tempers erupted. Scofield threatened Blake with physical violence. Blake became enraged. Here, in the poet's words, is what happened next: "I . . . took him by the Elbows & pushed him before me till I had got him out. There I intended to have left him. But he turning about put himself into a Posture of Defiance threatening & swearing at me. I perhaps foolishly & perhaps not, stepped out at the Gate

& putting aside his blows, took him again by the Elbows & keeping his back to me pushed him forwards down the road about fifty yards he all the while endeavouring to turn round & strike me & raging & cursing which drew out several neighbours."

Publicly shamed and vengeful, Scofield charged Blake with treason. He claimed that the engraver had damned the king and called "all soldiers . . . slaves." Taking Scofield seriously, the local authorities arrested Blake. Hayley kindly bailed him out, but Blake, terrified for his life, was later put on trial at Chichester. Fortunately, with Hayley's help, and after Scofield's questionable character was revealed, Blake was acquitted and soon back in London.

This wasn't the only time Blake's wrath flared in public. When he perceived tyranny in any guise, he became fiercely bellicose. But of the many forms that Blake's righteous pugnacity took, the poetic was the most prevalent. With his art, he warred against oppression. In his preface to *Milton*, Blake calls for a "Bow of burning gold," "Arrows of desire," a "Spear," and a "Chariot of fire." Armed and vehement, he makes his vow: "I will not cease from Mental Fight . . . // Till we have built Jerusalem, / In Englands green & pleasant Land."

Blake's poetry is aggressive, a verbal assault inspiring antagonistic responses: the strife of creation. To read, to perceive, as Blake prescribes, requires the almost impossible destruction of a lifetime of protective thought and a courageous exposure to unruly powers. Proper composing necessitates the same: each moment to fight against all that you said the instant before, to attack yourself constantly, to annihilate your draft and start anew.

Blake called these constant labors mental war. In contrast to "corporeal" battling, imaginative skirmishing challenges unjust abstractions. For Blake, this mindful struggling is the highest state we can achieve. Blake's true Eden, recall, is not the earthly paradise where contraries take respite from their mutually rewarding struggles. Eden is instead the imagination creatively sparring, laboring to generate specifically human forms that raise us above our merely natural cravings — forms like charity, which requires that we empathize with the suffering of another, or art, where we envision cities or poems or paintings that cultivate elegant generosity.

To be east of Eden, fallen irreparably, is to live in fear of these battles of imagination and to grip, out of fear, predictability, security, stasis. Those who stiffen to this inertia, those who are afraid to take the risks required for creation, are obsessed with the worst part of themselves, their "Spectre." The Spectre is ratio *in extremis*: the reason bent on totally dominating its environment. The Spectre holds hierarchy above polarity, favoring one side of any antinomy and demeaning or annihilating the other. As such, the Spectre is depraved Urizen, Blake's figure for reason, who dreams of a "solid without fluctuation" and a "joy without pain." In this terrible reverie, form is better than energy; reason trumps emotion; order rules over contingency. But without polarity, everything dies. Only waste remains, desert or ice. (Fittingly, Mary Shelley's *Frankenstein* begins and ends in the frozen Arctic. Victor, the hero, hates death and tries to destroy it in favor of life. In suppressing one side of the necessary opposition between living and dying, though, he ends up making a death machine, a monster that turns lively loved ones into corpses.)

The Spectre is the "Selfhood," a "false body," an "Incrustation over" the "Immortal / Spirit." The Self is false because it negates contraries and is thus utterly divorced from life. To dwell in the Selfhood is solipsistic, to be secluded in an unyielding carapace of abstractions. In this enclosure

(Blake calls it the "Mundane Shell"), we believe we are acting when in fact we are doing nothing at all. As Blake ex-
plains, "To hinder another is not an act; it is the contrary;
it is a restraint on action both in ourselves & in the person
hinder'd, for he who hinders another omits his own duty at
the same time. Murder is hindering another. Theft is Hindering Another. Backbiting, Undermining, Circumventing
& whatever is Negative is Vice."

If we are obsessed with rational control—of people and
things—then we value only what fits within our predetermined perceptual categories, fanatical and adamantine.
When we are mentally dictatorial in this way, a person or
thing is only significant to us either as a supporter of our
tightly held networks or as a threat. Any characteristics beyond these two are meaningless. These regulatory abstractions thus negate a person or thing's particularity and freedom. But in imposing these administrative concepts we
aren't acting at all, even if we think we are. We are in fact
reducing ourselves and those we want to manage into units
in a static system—as intellectual tyrants we must behave
in predictable ways and view our subjects mechanistically as
well. Imprisoning others incarcerates the jailer.

To "act," to work, to create, to enter into spiritual warfare, is to cast off the Spectre, the Selfhood, and to "cleanse"
the "Spirit by self-examination / To bathe in the Waters of
Life." This means living so that you hinder as few creatures
as possible. "The most sublime act is to set another before
you." While there is certainly an ethic behind this—an em-
phasis on benevolence—there is also implied a prescription
for creativity. To set another before you can mean, behave
selflessly, but it can also signify this: constantly set something against yourself that opposes your present conclu-
sions, comfortable and probably egocentric, and awakens
you to otherness, to influence beyond your immediate
grasp, muses inspiring new expressions and gestures, endless and rewarding labor.

No one labored at his art more diligently than Blake. That his last shilling was spent on a pencil for sketching Dante's shades and that his final act was to draw his wife — these events point to Blake's lifelong habit of working almost every waking hour almost every day of the week, even during holidays. According to one young man who visited the older Blake, the poet said, "I never stop for anything; I work on, whether ill or not."

Much of this work was not for remuneration but in service of his visions. Blake's commissions for engraving jobs decreased as his life advanced, partly because his designs were considered odd by the booksellers, and in part because he got a reputation for being dilatory, but mostly because he was too consumed by his poetic creations to put much thought into his business.

With little gainful employment, the elder Blake lived in grim poverty; many of his guests noted his scantily furnished home, his near-empty cupboard, and his worn, dirty clothes. But the dirt was not filth. It was the stain of labor, oil and ink and paint. A story about J. M. W. Turner is instructive. Once a visitor called on the great artist, saying he was a painter. Turner demanded the man to show his hands, and found that they were immaculately clean. Turner then whispered to an assistant: "Turn the fellow out. He's no artist."

Blake's art grew from daily, gritty, grinding work. Though he often claimed that his poems and designs just appeared in his head, complete and delivered from eternity, he nonetheless spent his hours toiling, in close quarters, among greasy copper plates, foul-smelling corrosives, and black solutions that clotted his pores. The printing process proffered little rest, requiring the continual inking, priming, and cleaning of the plates as well as the painstaking labor of painting on the small metal rectangles. And Blake did all of this, frequently for sixteen hours a day, out of passion more than necessity, so enkindled was he with his vision. "Exuberance is beauty," he once wrote: a paean to his own mighty and noble endurance.

Blake emphasized the importance of activity at least as much as he praised imagination. For him, exertion and imagination were little different: both had as their lofty end the creation of humanizing art. As we have seen, he proclaimed that "*Energy* is an eternal delight." To this he added, "he who desires, but acts not, breeds pestilence." For Blake, lack of fervor was a sin far worse than active evil. Men get to heaven, he wrote, "not because they have curbed and govern'd their passions or have no passions but because they have cultivated their Understandings." Though we can't take the following line with entire seriousness—it's spoken by a prejudiced, hyperbolic devil in *The Marriage of Heaven and Hell*—it still firmly urges Blake's hatred of repressed zeal: "sooner murder an infant in its crib than nurse unacted desires." "Mere enthusiasm is the all in all," he more reasonably stated. "Passion and expression are Beauty Itself." "The Desire of Man being Infinite, the possession is Infinite, and himself Infinite."

Without his abounding desire to create, and create more, Blake probably would have folded in the face of poverty and neglect. But he didn't, and in this there is heroism. As Peter Ackroyd puts it, in Blake's "lifelong career of arduous labour there is something grander and more heroic than the lucubrations of the Lakeside poets," those brooding figures in England's watery north, Coleridge and Wordsworth and Southey.

There is nothing romantic about Blake's creative process or any other. You set your alarm. You get up in the dark and grope toward the coffee. Juiced on caffeine, you bang out five-hundred words. They're not your best; you'll fix them later. You keep writing. If the writing comes too easily, trash it. Sometimes, after weeks of grueling labor, you find the right first line. Celebrate for a moment, and then move to the next task. You're only as good, you sadly realize, as the sentence you're writing.

Industry is all there is. To lose yourself in it, to become it, its boundless but rugged promises, its oceans of tone and form, rimed now with rough ice, and then freshened by the warm trades: this is grace.

To sacrifice life for art is to embody the "Eternal Great Humanity Divine." This is Eden, where ceaseless mental battle produces aesthetic concords — "Wheel within Wheel [which] in freedom revolve in harmony and peace" — that run counter to the ugly machinery of institutionalized ratio: "wheel without wheel, with cogs tyrannic moving by compulsion each other." When you are fully engaged in this creative warfare, lost in robust activity, you forget all about your temporal limitations, your burdensome past and disquieting future. You get so involved in what you're doing, that when you look up at the clock, hours have passed, though you feel that you've been at work only minutes. This is Eternity — not endless time or static timelessness but the "Period the Poet's Work is Done," the "Eternal Now," the "pulsation" that "Satan cannot find."

So often we are troubled by past and future, and thus alienated from the present moment. I sit at my computer on a Wednesday morning and try to write. But my attention keeps straying to what has happened earlier in my life, maybe two years ago, perhaps ten minutes, those events toward which I nostalgically long or from which I regretfully recoil. Also I anticipate an appointment to which I've been looking forward or dread an upcoming responsibility. Dissipated by these feelings, I hover in a ghostly limbo, composed of apparitions of a past that is no more and haunts of a future not yet here. While drifting among these abstractions, I'm not really living. I'm overly self-conscious, obsessed with my personal history, my success, my failures. I can't get out of myself, connect to something beyond, something "not me." I've imprisoned myself in a ratio of my own making, egotism's same dull round: wherever I look, there I am. Distant from this life — right here, right now, this instant — and perversely enamored of monotony, of death, I can't write anything worth keeping. I don't know what to do. I just know I've got to kill time, somehow.

The problem is "lag." That is what Ken Kesey called the division between what's actually happening and how our mind responds to what's happening. The most basic lag, Kesey thought — at least according to Tom Wolfe in *Electric Kool-Aid Test* — "is the sensory lag, the lag between the time your senses receive something and you are able to react. One-thirtieth of a second is the time it takes, if you're the most alert person alive, and most people are a lot slower than that." And so none of us, no matter how alert, can overcome this temporal gap. We "are all of us doomed to spend our lives watching a movie of our lives — we are always acting on what has just finished happening. It happened at least 1/30th of a second ago. We think we're in the present, but we aren't."

Sadly, there are more troublesome lags that distance us even further from the present: "There are historical and social lags, where people are living by what their ancestors or somebody else perceived, and they may be twenty-five or fifty years or centuries behind, and nobody can be creative without overcoming all those lags first of all." Through education, a person can overcome these obvious lags, "but he's still going to be up against one of the worst lags of all, the psychological. Your emotions remain behind because of training, education, the way you were brought up, blocks, hang-ups and stuff like that, and as a result your mind wants to go one way but your emotions don't."

Kesey thought that psychotropic drugs might enable us to cross the lag and slip into the now. Certainly Aldous Huxley in his Blake-inspired *The Doors of Perception* suggested this possibility. But aren't there certain moments in life when we — clear of drugs and sober as judges — maybe through luck, or perhaps because of long practice or intentional disposition, feel as though we are in the "now," even if we might indeed be 1/30 second behind? We've all had these moments, these "delicious awakenings," as Emerson calls them, and they are the climaxes of our lives.

―――

On another morning, for no reason I can account for, there's no time to kill at all — not because there's not enough of it, but because temporality disappears from my attention. I start my writing with a sentence, the one I've been hoping for, and then I lose myself in the current of the words that follow. I get in the zone; I find my groove; I'm on my game. This is absolute immersion in what I'm doing. This is what psychologists now call "flow." Self-awareness fades and with it my attention to the clock. No more do I "look before and after" and "pine for what is not" — to use Shelley's phrasing. I am here, now, enjoying perfect concord between my expertise and my task, delighting in the interplay between discipline and spontaneity. I am concentrating intensely but feel no strain. I am relaxed but dynamic. The sentences come and they come, each one distinct and elegant yet in harmony with the overall intention. I continue to write. After a while, when I feel my interest wane, I look at my watch. Two hours have passed, though the whole episode, to me, seemed only moments. Time has flown by, as though it didn't even exist. I turn to the words. I read them. They are unexpected yet lucid, provocative and shining. I hit the save button.

I was in eternity and did my poet's work. It came like a melody from a cardinal or the falling of mountain water. Now we understand why Blake frequently claimed that his art came to him through divine inspiration, that he was merely the vehicle of spirit. He no doubt reveled in the flow. Describing the origin of an early poem, he said, "My Fairy set upon my table and dictated Europe." Another time, he captured the explosive power of this kind of visitation, an eruption of language: "When I am commanded by the Spirits, then I write, and the moment I have written, I see the words fly about the room in all directions. It is then published." He came to count on his imperious muse. Speaking of an epic he was planning to write, he claimed that "[t]his Poem shall by Divine Assistance be progressively Printed & Ornamented with Prints & given to the Public." He talked of his poem *Milton* in the same way: "I have written this poem from immediate Dictation, twelve or sometimes twenty or thirty lines at a time, without Premeditation and even against my Will; the Time it has taken in writing was thus rendered Non Existent, and an immense Poem Exists which seems to be the Labor of a long Life, all produced without Labor or Study."

Dictation is the act of transcribing the words of another. When we are inspired, immersed in the mellifluous flux of the present and pouring forth purified words, we feel as though we are indeed writing down immortal sentences, finished and voiced to us from some gorgeous beyond.

Whether Blake's poetry was really heaven-sent or simply a product of his blessed liberation from self-awareness is of course beyond our ken. What we do grasp, though, are the lessons intimated by his descriptions of divine dictation: open your heart, listen to its convictions, and the right words will come; to try too hard to write well is to write badly; too much conscious straining toward a goal prohibits the fulfillment.

This was Blake's faith: wait, patiently, and the muse will always come, bringing lines ready-made, stanzas done in full. Surely this belief is an extremely important and perhaps essential part of the creative process because it calms those anxieties over writers' block, anxieties that can perpetuate themselves, intensify, and eventually shut down composition for months or years.

We've all been there. The ideas just aren't there, and, instead of relaxing into the conviction that they will soon come again, we whip up the worry. We fear that they might never come back. This anxiety causes increasing pressure to create: we say, I will write today, damn it, if it's the last thing I do. But this strain does the exact opposite of what we want. Clouding our minds and agitating our hearts, it hinders that blending of focus and looseness we need to write effectively and so only makes the obstacles between us and successful expression more imposing. And so we suffer even more stress, and thus try harder, and therefore strengthen the block, and before too long just exhaust ourselves into a frustrated stasis.

To avoid this paralysis we must trust the weirdness, knowing that those uncanny hints and strange radiances will eventually, whether we expect them or will them or not, appear, like phantoms, and haunt our minds with new visions and unforeseen words. Having this faith, we don't press. Not pressing, we hold open a serene space for the productive spookiness to arise, for the unsettling wisps that pervade the familiar with the bizarre and the outré with familiarity. Shivered into this middle world, simply given to us, as from a magical realm, we are now ready to write.

Jung once said that "religion is a defense against the experience of God." Eugen Herrigel, author of *Zen in the Art of Archery*, would agree. Too much systematic effort toward an end ensures failure: "The more obstinately you try to learn how to shoot the arrow for the sake of hitting the goal, the less you will succeed in the one and the further the other will recede." Almost every Little League pitcher knows this. If he aims the ball at the catcher's mitt, he'll miss it; the only way to hit the mark—just throw the ball.

This is the problem with the overly self-conscious quest, be it for the divine, the bull's-eye, the third strike, or a well-turned phrase: the ego gets in the way. If I am too aware of what I'm doing, then I'm splitting myself in two—into spectator and doer. The spectator—my third eye, invisible, that monitors and often criticizes my deeds—cannot stay focused on the task at hand. It wanders and broods, perhaps unfavorably comparing this immediate event to past ones or picturing negative effects in the future. Whatever this suspended ego thinks, it is motivated by fear and desire— desire for a pleasing prize, fear of going without. These impulses make me question what I'm doing. I second-guess myself. I get all blocked up. I'm frustrated, uninspired, a failure.

Blake had this kind of fatigue in mind when he wrote, "If the *Sun and Moon* should doubt, / They'd immediately go out." For him, the opposite of self-destructive doubt, creativity, emerges only when egotistical drudgery subsides. Then the writer (or the seeker or the pitcher or the archer) becomes receptive to the unexpected, ready to be inspired—breathed into by unforeseen endowments he could not predict or even hope for, since he didn't before know the nature of their force.

But as Herrigel makes clear, though the miraculous instance transcends progressive preparation, only diligent training prepares us for the gift. Assiduous, sometimes desperate effort, days and years of it, is the well-turned soil out of which the sentences and gestures grow green and luminous. The master archer and the poet improvise beautifully, but they have mastered their crafts through long, awkward struggle. The dancer's spontaneous leaps, natural as antelopes, have bloody toes and sprained ankles to thank. Decades of training govern Pollock's seemingly random splatters. Precise practice, technical as machinery, guides Michael Jordan's whimsical dexterity. The monk must pray for a whole life—there are bruises on his knees—before the holy hour. Keats might have said that if "poetry comes not as naturally as the leaves to a tree, it had better not come at all." But he also knew that the poet's soul comes from lengthy suffering: "Do you not see," he asks, "how necessary a world of pains and troubles is to school an intelligence and make it a soul?" Nietzsche also knew this. Ill from overwork yet eager for mental flight, he proclaimed: "He who would learn to fly one day must first learn to stand and walk and run and climb and dance; one cannot fly into flying."

Dictation has another meaning. While the word can signify serene transcription, it also betokens a stern command, possibly arbitrary and cruel. Dictation in this sense counters compositional grace; strained obedience typifies this darker side of the term. But for the writer, servitude can't be separated from the smoothness. He must be enslaved by the capricious muse if this goddess is to grant him, when he least expects it, her bounty.

Blake's blackened hands and eyes red and swollen from the fumes that precipitated his death; his weary days painting minute words, in reverse, on copper plates; his sedulous study of the Bible and his efforts to educate himself in the most difficult philosophies; his endurance of failure and neglect; his debilitating bouts with "Nervous Fear"; his own inevitable addiction to ratios, to labyrinthine mythological systems; his glimpses of real madness; his grief over his dead brother Robert; his commercial ventures, unsuccessful; his hunger for bread and cheese — all of these woes had to be there, cut into his heart, to welcome those impetuous raptures when his words and images, unasked for and barely anticipated, sparked lightning in his brain.

Creation is an *agon* between egotism and generosity. Blake's shorthand for narcissism is "Jealousy." When we are jealous, we are stuck in a perverse fantasy of absolute ownership, believing that another is our property and thus off-limits to all others but ourselves. Jealousy exists in another guise as well, equally selfish — envy of someone's success that drives us to hope for that person's downfall. The logic goes: if I can't have what he's got, then he shouldn't have it either; let me hinder him however I can, bring him down to my level.

The path out of this hatred is "Forgiveness," Blake's synonym for a legitimate act: not hindering another through selfish judgments but instead suspending condemnation and simply letting it all be. This charitable perspective toward the world, a respite, however brief, from the self-consciousness that impedes self and other alike, empowers us to see the wondrous complexity of the universe and motivates us to conjure aesthetic structures appropriate to the vision.

To forgive is to create, to find Eden: "Mutual Forgiveness of each Vice, / Such are the Gates of Paradise." It is also Eternity, where the law is: "each shall mutually / Annihilate himself for others good."

This is Blake's abiding paradox. One must renounce herself to find herself, give away everything to get it all, annihilate her personality to become truly human. This fulfilling self-renunciation, the origin of poetry or painting, is the "fourfold."

In a letter to a friend, Blake wrote this verse:

> Now I fourfold vision see
> And a fourfold vision is given me
> Tis fourfold in my supreme delight
> And threefold in soft Beulahs night
> And twofold Always. May God us keep
> From Single vision & Newtons sleep.

These lines suggest that there are four ways of experiencing the world, each dependent upon a particular psychological disposition.

One way is the "Single vision & Newtons sleep," the reduction of matter to abstract quantities moving predictably in empty space. This perspective is single because it ignores the dynamic contraries, flattening multifariously conflicted creatures to uniform concepts.

The twofold agitates this monotony.

> A frowning Thistle implores my stay
> What to others a trifle appears
> Fills me full of smiles or tears
> For double the vision my Eyes do see
> And a double vision is always with me
> With my inward Eye 'tis an old Man grey
> With my outward a Thistle across my way.

The twofold occurs when we are sensitive to animated nature. When we are in this mood, beings inspire in us an acute emotional response that in turn stokes our imaginations into symbol-making. The world in this case is neither an obstacle to be surmounted with reason nor an insignificant collection of distant objects hardly worth our attention. Instead, the earth is alive, polarized, pregnant with significance: light mixes with darkness and objects mingle with subjects. Mysterious thistles turn into wise old men or the finch, so distant, into a holy poet.

If the single vision produces Ulro, the twofold vision propagates Generation. The threefold way of seeing begets Beulah, the region of lunar reverie. In this state, there is no effort to perceive nature as it is and then transform it into images laden with emotion. Rather, the eye rises above the ground and on the horizon projects seductive phantoms never witnessed on earth—fairies or dragons or unicorns or undying gardens or pale magic maidens or knights that pine. Magic seems to happen in this soft delusional realm where the contraries come to rest. A kind of bliss prevails. But this bower of haunts is also a lotus-dose, a siren song. It is in fact where the sexes languish in unfulfilled erotic longing. Divorced from nature's vexed vitality, weakened by unrequited desire, we can atrophy at the threefold. Under Beulah, remember, is Ulro.

The fourfold—the level of vision, genius, the human, Eden, and Eternity—subsumes the other three ways of seeing, each partial, and comprehends compelling wholeness. When we perceive the world as fourfold, we grasp each event as a site of infinite relationship, a gathering, in an intricate dance, of agitated atoms, animated polarities, fantasies extremely luscious, and revelations of the imagination's potential.

I watch a fly zigzagging near my window. I am attuned to its thrilling materiality, its darting minuteness. But I also apprehend the insect as a living creature, with heart and brain, and I conceive a symbol: the fly hovering over the corpse as life rising from death. At this instant, my fancy elevates above my immediate environment—the fly tacking in the September brightness—and floats in a daydream nostalgic for something gone, dead to me: a daffodil pressed in a book or a girlfriend moved away. Encompassing these levels all together, I feel the fullness of being, rococo and roundness, fierce talons and benevolence. The fly is everything: an electrifying green-blue blur; a marriage of my mind and matter; a place where yearning invokes beauty; and a revelation of

the innumerable ways I can relate to this or any other holy
creature. All this happens at once, this fourfold realization,
with much or perhaps all of the intuition occurring beyond
self-consciousness, too quick for the ratio or Satan to grab.

Blake expresses the fourfold in other ways. In *Four Zoas*,
an epic he never finished, he depicts the imaginative human
as a harmonious merger of Urthona, Luvah, Tharmas, and
Urizen, intimating, respectively, imagination, feeling, sensation, and reason. Working together, these four faculties perpetually generate art. The sensations of Tharmas produce
Luvah's emotional reactions that in turn inspire Urthona
to create images, images that achieve their greatest force
within Urizen's elegant boundaries. When this synthesis occurs, Albion, Blake's figure for the universal human, pros-
pers. But of course this synthesis is all too rare, for generally
Urizen tries to take charge of the other Zoas and in doing
so fragments them. This is the fall: reason aspiring to superi-
ority and establishing the ratio as the only proper mode of
perception and then demeaning imagination, emotion, and
sensation.

But in the end, the numerical rendering of wholeness,
though it connotes the totality we feel when we create,
is, as Blake well knew, rather rigid. Perhaps his other, less
systematic descriptions of compositional plenitude come
closer, like when he in the *Book of Urizen* describes the lithe
rhythms of genesis.

> Earth was not: nor globes of attraction
> The will of the Immortal expanded
> Or contracted his all flexible senses.
> Death was not, but eternal life sprung.

"More! More! is the cry of a mistaken soul, less than
All cannot satisfy Man." So Blake wrote early in his career.
Around the same time, he proclaimed that "the road to ex-

cess leads to the palace of wisdom," for "you never know what is enough unless you know what is more than enough." The first statement expresses one of Blake's main assumptions — if we are not possessed of the infinite, we can never be satisfied. But the second suggests the impossibility of having it all: beyond enough, beyond alleged fullness, there's always more. This is the paradoxical nature of the infinite: an experience of it shows us that we can't have an experience of it.

This is the fourfold's revelation. Immersing ourselves in our writing, we enter so deeply into time, into the present, that we transcend temporality to eternity, and we descend so profoundly into space, into presence, that we go beyond space to the infinite. Such is the exuberance of writing, the ecstasy. But eternity and infinity are inexhaustible, never totally within the circle of our cognition. There's always more to undergo, more to write. The work is never done, though we are complete each instant. This is the writer's creed: "Enough! Or Too Much!"

"If a thing loves, it is infinite." All of Blake is here. To love anything, from a daughter to a speckled wren to a sonnet, is to respond enthusiastically to its unprecedented particularity, irreducible to any one representation, boundless in its relations to itself and to others, in the ways it metamorphoses and unendingly divides. Exposing ourselves to a creature's abundant possibilities, we in loving realize our own infinite potentials for connection, for change, for involvement. Enlightened, we as lovers also understand that love's labor is never over — that affection, to persist, must be as limitless as its origin and object.

To write well is to adore the bright line, the translucent sentence that reveals what is true, right now, about this one thing. What is true is that this being is *this* self-contained entity and nothing else besides. But within the boundaries of the thing's area and volume are countless minute particulars that themselves differentiate into further infinitesimal particles and these do the same, and so on, interminably. And so writing with excellence is loving not just the line but also what escapes design, always just beyond semantics and syntax, trope and tractate. Lively writing requires nothing less than a passion, perverse maybe, for the fragment bereft of finish, hunger beyond filling, constant privation.

In *Moby-Dick*, Melville writes, "God keep me from ever completing anything. This whole book is but a draught — nay, but a draught of a draught. Oh, Time, Strength, Cash, and Patience!" Dickinson agrees: "Finite — to fail, but infinite to Venture — ." Both approach James Joyce's *Finnegans Wake*, whose first sentence completes the last and whose final sentence begins the first, and so a volume that begins where it ends and concludes where it starts, a work whose words never stop turning and so they write forever and must always be read.

Blake's own texts—irreducible to systemization, resilient to abstraction, seductively bewildering, abysmal—are like the *Wake*. They proliferate infinite interpretations, unfathomable labors. To create like Blake necessitates similar sublimities, words that are bottomless and lines that don't stop saying. The composing is frustrating. It is exuberant.

The Blakean mood for creating is well-intimated by a German term, *Sehnsucht*. The word usually translates as "longing," and it points to a sharp yearning for an inaccessible object. This pining, though painful, is also ecstatic, for it is a perpetual contemplation of the desired thing, an earnest gaze on what, if ever grasped, would bring consummate bliss. When we feel this kind of ache, we are ardent for being inconsolable. We hold adoringly to the emptiness.

C. S. Lewis, whose novel *The Great Divorce* is a long response to *The Marriage of Heaven and Hell*, claims that this sort of infinite longing is joy. In *Surprised by Joy*, a memoir, Lewis says that the primary theme in his life has been "an unsatisfied desire which is itself more desirable than any other satisfaction. I call it Joy, which is here a technical term and must be sharply distinguished both from Happiness and from Pleasure. Joy (in my sense), has indeed one characteristic, and one only, in common with them; the fact that anyone who has experienced it will want it again. Apart from that, and considered only in its quality, it might almost equally well be called a particular kind of unhappiness or grief. But then it is a kind we want. I doubt whether anyone who has tasted it would ever, if both were in his power, exchange it for all the pleasures in the world. But then Joy is never in our power and pleasure often is."

Lewis characterizes this joy as that "unnameable something, desire for which pierces us like a rapier at the smell of bonfire, the sound of wild ducks flying overhead, the title of *The Well at the End of the World*, the opening lines of 'Kubla

Khan,' the morning cobwebs in late summer, or the noise of falling waves."

Blake would call this joy, vision: when we are sunk in the present but adrift in inexhaustible promise, sated yet parched. There is a danger to this way of living. It might tempt us into demeaning time and its animated productions in favor of hoping always for something else, far away. And vision can conversely cause bitterness toward an infinity that can never be attained and a lust, sullen and crude, for nature's limits. But ideally, Blake's theory of vision engenders the revelation that Blake enjoyed during his last earthly hour, when the muse that helped to kill him animated him yet once more: the earth's inevitable ravages, its ruinous poisons, might murder us, but it is precisely time's annihilations that create the bounteousness of life. Manure nurtures the posy. The fever's flush is ecstatic strangeness. Unrequited longing engenders the imagination's plenitude. Our most anxious fears birth their solace, their transcendence: sublime paintings that assuage and poems boundlessly alive.

ACKNOWLEDGMENTS

I would most like to thank the man to whom this book is dedicated, Robert D. Richardson, Jr. He gave me the idea for this book and encouraged me throughout the writing process. This is but one of the many times Bob has generously supported my endeavors. I also appreciate several friends from whom I've over the years gleaned much wisdom about writing and living: John McNally, Philip Kuberski, Dennis Sampson, Philip Arnold, Steve Jeck, Ken Cooper, Andy Lester-Niles, and Jennifer Blevins. I'm also thankful for the recent Blakean conversations I've been privileged to have with two of the most thrilling intellectuals I've ever met: Michael Murphy and Jeffrey Kripal, both of whom blew my mind at the Esalen Institute one summer. I feel very fortunate to be publishing with the University of Iowa Press; Joseph Parsons has been a fabulous editor from beginning to end, and Jonathan Haas copyedited my book with great precision and skill. Finally, as always, I'm deeply appreciative of my wife, Sandi, and my daughter, Una. They both perpetually assuage my nervous fears and connect me to the infinite possibilities of real affection.

Many works of brilliant Blake scholarship have made this little book possible. I'd here like to note those that most prominently shaped the book, directly and indirectly: Alexander Gilchrist's *The Life of William Blake* (London: Hesperides Press, 2008); Algernon Charles Swinburne's *Blake: A Critical Essay* (London: John Camden, 1868); Northrop Frye's *Fearful Symmetry: A Study of William Blake* (Princeton, NJ: Princeton University Press, 1947); David V. Erdman's *Blake: Prophet against Empire* (Princeton, NJ: Princeton University Press, 1954); Kathleen Raine's *Blake and Tradition* (Princeton, NJ: Bollingen Press of Princeton University Press, 1968); Hazard Adams's *Blake and Yeats: The Contrary Vision* (New York: Russell and Russell, 1968); Harold Bloom's *Blake's Apocalypse: A Study in Poetic Argument* (Ithaca, NY: Cornell University Press, 1970); Joseph Anthony Wittreich's *Angel of Apocalypse: Blake's Idea of Milton* (Madison, WI: University of Wisconsin Press, 1975); Donald Ault's *Visionary Physics: Blake's Response to Newton* (Chicago, IL: University of Chicago Press, 1976); Diana Hume George's *Blake and Freud* (Ithaca, NY: Cornell University Press, 1980); Morris Eaves's *William Blake's Theory of Art* (Princeton, NJ: Princeton University Press, 1982); S. Foster Damon's *A Blake Dictionary: The Ideas and Symbols of William Blake* (Providence, RI: Brown University Press, 1988); Vincent Arthur de Luca's *Words of Eternity: Blake and the Poetics of the Sublime* (Princeton, NJ: Princeton University Press, 1991); Jeanne Moskal's *Blake, Ethics, and Forgiveness* (Tuscaloosa, AL: University of Alabama Press, 1994); E. P. Thompson's *Witness against the Beast: William Blake and the Moral Law* (New York: The Free Press, 1995); Peter Ackroyd's *Blake: A Biography* (New York: Ballantine, 1997); Mark Lussier's *Romantic Dynamics: The Poetics of Physicality* (New York: Palgrave, 1999); Kevin Hutchings's *Imagining Nature: Blake's Environmental Poetics* (Montreal: McGill-Queens University Press, 2003); G. E. Bentley's *Stranger from Paradise:*

A Biography of William Blake (London: Paul Mellon Centre for British Art, 2003); Marsha Keith Schuchard's *Why Mrs. Blake Cried: William Blake and the Sexual Basis of Spiritual Vision* (London: Century, 2006); and Jeffrey J. Kripal's "Reality Against Society: Blake, Antinomianism, and the American Counterculture," *Common Knowledge* 31:1 (2007), 89–112.

BE AN ARTIST

"Stay, Kate . . . angel to me": Alexander Gilchrist, *The Life of William Blake* (London: Hesperides Press, 2008), p. 352.

"I have . . . in Paradise": *Blake Records*, ed. G. E. Bentley (Oxford: Clarendon Press, 1969), p. 221.

"I have been . . . Foolish Body decays": William Blake, *The Complete Poetry and Prose of William Blake*, ed. David V. Erdman (New York: Doubleday, 1988), p. 785. [Hereafter cited as *CPP*.]

"Blake . . . there is felicity": Henry Crabb Robinson, *Blake, Coleridge, Wordsworth, Lamb, Etc.: Being Selections from the Remains of Henry Crabb Robinson* (Ithaca, NY: Cornell University Press, 2010), p. 4.

"I must Create . . . to Create": *CPP*, p. 153.

"To create. . . labour of ages": *CPP*, p. 37.

"Degrade first the Arts . . . Mankind degrade": *CPP*, p. 635.

"Jesus . . . only God": Robinson, p. 3.

"Man . . . Imaginative Vision": *CPP*, p. 663.

"The imagination . . . Existence itself": *CPP*, p. 132.

CONTRARIES

"Ah, Sun-flower . . . is done": *CPP*, p. 25.

"I've . . . God": Michael Schumacher, *Dharma Lion: A Critical Biography of Allen Ginsberg* (New York: St. Martin's, 1994), p. 96.

"I . . . in it": Schumacher, p. 96.

"Since art is . . . true art": Barry Miles, *Ginsberg: A Biography* (New York: Harper Collins, 1990), p. 47.

"Energy . . . Delight": *CPP*, p. 34.
"To Generalize . . . Distinction of Merit": *CPP*, p. 641.
"Without Contraries . . . no progression": *CPP*, p. 34.
"Mental": *CPP*, p. 95.

THE RATIO
"Born like a Garden . . . Sown": *CPP*, p. 656.
"As a man . . . Sees": *CPP*, p. 702.
"ratio": *CPP*, p. 2.
"Daughters of Memory": *CPP*, p. 95.
"repeat the same . . . over again": *CPP*, p. 3.
"an Innumerable . . . God Almighty": *CPP*, p. 566.
"He who sees . . . only": *CPP*, p. 3.
"Natural Objects . . . to do with Memory": *CPP*, p. 666.

MINUTE PARTICULARS
"He who sees . . . God": *CPP*, p. 3.
"a tree . . . bough like stars": Gilchrist, p. 6.
"Nervous Fear": *CPP*, p. 708.
"doors of perception . . . cleansed": *CPP*, p. 39.
"sensual enjoyment": *CPP*, p. 39.
"World . . . Grain of Sand": *CPP*, p. 493.
"Bird that cuts . . . world of delight": *CPP*, p. 35.
"Fable or Allegory . . . All that Exists": *CPP*, p. 554.
"Singular & Particular . . . the Sublime": *CPP*, p. 647.
"plea of the scoundrel . . . flatterer": *CPP*, p. 205.
"many-colored geometries . . . ultimate revelation": Aldous
    Huxley, *The Doors of Perception and Heaven and Hell* (New
    York: Harper Perennial Modern Classics, 2009), p. 15.
"naked existence": Huxley, p. 17.
"seeing what Adam . . . his creation": Huxley, p. 17.
"mathematical abstraction . . . quivering": Huxley, p. 17.
"could never . . . all existence": Huxley, p. 18.
"Leave out . . . chaos again": *CPP*, p. 550.
"Precision of pencil . . . Nothing": *CPP*, p. 657.

"Not Human . . . Rational Demonstration": *CPP*, p. 142.

"the fallacy . . . concreteness": Alfred North Whitehead, *Science and the Modern World* (New York: Free Press, 1997), p. 51.

"simple location": Whitehead, *Science*, pp. 49–52.

"The Loss of Creature": Walker Percy, *The Message in the Bottle: How Queer Man Is, How Queer Language Is, and What One Has to Do with the Other* (New York: Picador, 2000), pp. 46–54.

LOOKING

"I know . . . its Powers": *CPP*, p. 702.

"*Esse est percipi*": Frye, pp. 22–25.

"Where man . . . barren": *CPP*, p. 38.

"where . . . am lost": Martin Buber, *I and Thou*, trans. Walter Kaufmann (New York: Touchstone, 1971), p. 70.

"[g]enius . . . unhabitual way": William James, *Principles of Psychology*, vol. 2 (New York: Dover, 1950), p. 110.

"My Business . . . Circumference": Emily Dickinson, *Emily Dickinson: Selected Letters*, ed. Thomas H. Johnson (Cambridge, MA: Belknap Press of Harvard University Press, 1986), p. 176.

"I Dwell . . . Prose": Emily Dickinson, *The Poems of Emily Dickinson: Reading Edition*, ed. R. W. Franklin (Cambridge, MA: Belknap Press of Harvard University Press, 2005), p. 46.

"Damn . . . relaxes": *CPP*, p. 37.

"Turn the eyes . . . twenty years!": Ralph Waldo Emerson, *Emerson: Selected Essays*, ed. Larzer Ziff (New York: Penguin, 1982), p. 30.

"spear of summer grass": Walt Whitman, *The Portable Walt Whitman*, ed. Michael Warner (New York: Penguin, 2003), p. 3.

"If you are . . . isn't expecting it": H. G. Wells, qtd. in Ralph Keyes, *The Courage to Write: How Writers Transcend Fears* (New York: Holt Paperbacks, 2003), p. 152.

COPY A GREAT DEAL

"pure sensation . . . forms and colours": Annie Dillard, *Pilgrim at Tinker Creek* (New York: Harper Perennial Modern Classics, 2007), p. 26.

"tormentingly difficult": Dillard, p. 27.

"dazzle of color-patches": Dillard, p. 27.

"tree with lights in it": Dillard, p. 28.

"been around . . . the peaches": Dillard, p. 29.

"dog at three fourteen . . . he saw them": Jorge Luis Borges, *Labyrinths*, eds. Donald A. Yates and James E. Irby, trans. André Maurois (New York: New Directions, 2007), p. 65.

"could continuously . . . intolerably exact": Borges, pp. 65–66.

"ferocious splendour": Borges, p. 66.

"almost incapable . . . diverse size and form": Borges, p. 65.

"was not . . . thought": Borges, p. 64.

"To think . . . only details": Borges, p. 64.

"The difference . . . Great Deal": *CPP*, p. 645.

"fulfill it": Matthew 5:17.

"Re-vision . . . act of survival": Adrienne Rich, *On Lies, Secrets, and Silence: Selected Prose, 1966–1978* (New York: Norton, 1995), p. 35.

"Until we can . . . afresh": Rich, p. 35.

"We need . . . hold over us": Rich, p. 35.

THE INFERNAL METHOD

"notion that man . . . doors of perception": *CPP*, p. 39.

"Loud sounds . . . ashes of the Dead": *CPP*, p. 100.

"The Divine hand . . . named Adam": *CPP*, p. 107.

"The nature of infinity . . . roll backward behind": *CPP*, p. 109.

"There is . . . Satan cannot find": *CPP*, p. 136.

"To touch . . . return": *CPP*, p. 123.

"The Wild Thyme . . . Eden": *CPP*, p. 136.

"That which . . . worth my care": *CPP*, p. 702.

"What was needed . . . seen through": Jerome McGann, "The Aim of Blake's Prophecies and the Uses of Blake Criticism," *Blake's Sublime Allegory*, ed. Joseph Anthony Wittreich and

Stuart Curran (Madison, WI: University of Wisconsin Press, 1973), p. 10.

"took precautions . . . writing": Walter Benjamin, qtd. in Susan Sontag, *Under the Sign of Saturn: Essays* (New York: Picador, 2002), p. 122.

"the veil of familiarity . . . of its forms": Percy Bysshe Shelley, *The Major Works*, eds. Zachary Leader and Michael O'Neill (Oxford: Oxford University Press, 2009), p. 698.

"no longer . . . infinity of languages": Roland Barthes, *S/Z: An Essay*, trans. Richard Miller (New York: Hill and Wang, 1975), p. 5.

"There is then . . . creative writing": Emerson, p. 90.

"I am . . . destroy the teacher": Whitman, p. 62.

POETRY UNFETTER'D

"first free-verse . . . English": William Blake, *The Complete Poems*, ed. Alicia Ostriker (New York: Penguin, 1978), p. 997.

"Monotonous Cadence . . . necessary to each other": *CPP*, pp. 145–46.

"Poetry Fetter'd . . . Race": *CPP*, p. 146.

"The Vegetative . . . Satanic Wheels": *CPP*, p. 157.

"Without Contraries . . . Evil is Hell": *CPP*, p. 34.

REVISING

"How admirable . . . fleeting": *The Essential Haiku: Versions of Bashō, Buson, and Issa*, ed. and trans. Robert Hass (New York: Ecco, 1995), p. 24.

"There are always . . . at first": Jacques Barzun, *Simple & Direct* (New York: Harper Perennial, 2001), p. 243.

"Forced to weigh . . . your style": Ursula K. Le Guin, *Steering the Craft: Exercises and Discussions on Story Writing for the Lone Navigator and the Mutinous Crew* (Portland, OR: Eighth Mountain Press, 1998), p. 147.

"Fiction does not . . . original and profound": John Gardner, *On Becoming a Novelist* (New York: Norton, 1999), p. 136.

"First drafts are shit": Ernest Hemingway, qtd. in Sol Stein, *Stein*

*on Writing: A Master Editor of Some of the Most Successful
Writers of Our Century Shares His Craft Techniques and
Strategies* (New York: St. Martin's Griffin, 2000), p. 277.

INNOCENCE

"Come in . . . you know": Gilchrist, p. 97.

"Unorganized Innocence . . . Ignorance": *CPP*, p. 96.

"And I . . . joy to hear": *CPP*, p. 7.

PLAY

"purposiveness without a purpose": Immanuel Kant, *Critique of
Judgment*, ed. Nicholas Walker, trans. James Creed Meredith
(Oxford: Oxford University Press, 2007), p. 57.

"no other . . . than *play*": Friedrich Nietzsche, *On the Genealogy
of Morals* and *Ecce Homo*, trans. Walter Kaufmann (New
York: Vintage, 1989), p. 256.

"a man's maturity . . . child at play": Friedrich Nietzsche, *Beyond
Good and Evil: Prelude to a Philosophy of the Future*, trans.
Marion Faber (Oxford: Oxford University Press, 2009), p. 62.

EXPERIENCE

"Energy . . . of Energy": *CPP*, p. 34.

"heard . . . fallen light renew!": *CPP*, p. 18.

"fearful symmetry": *CPP*, pp. 24–25.

"happy . . . heath": *CPP*, p. 22.

"honey from every wind": *CPP*, p. 6.

"happy copulation": *CPP*, p. 50.

"shall awaken . . . her chamber": *CPP*, p. 50.

"happy . . . wind": *CPP*, p. 50.

"not wholly unprovoked": Gilchrist, p. 315.

"patriarchal mood": Algernon Charles Swinburne, *Blake:
A Critical Essay* (London: John Camden, 1868), p. 16.

"Embraces are . . . the Feet": *CPP*, p. 223.

"The lust . . . of God": *CPP*, p. 36.

"require . . . Desire": *CPP*, pp. 474–75.

"He whose . . . wondrous Imaginations": *CPP*, p. 134.

"Enjoyment . . . food of Intellect": *CPP*, p. 700.

"What are called . . . spiritual world": Henry Crabb Robinson,
    p. 9.

"everything . . . is holy": *CPP*, p. 51.

GENERATION

"Life lives . . . one other": *CPP*, p. 369.

"point of mutual forgiveness . . . Lamb of God
    incomprehensible": *CPP*, p. 150.

"future generations . . . Most Sublime Poetry": *CPP*, p. 730.

"masterful images . . . shop of the heart": W. B. Yeats, *The
    Collected Poems of William Butler Yeats*, ed. Richard J.
    Finneran (New York: Scribners, 1996), pp. 347–48.

"a Deep Pit . . . reason for it": *CPP*, p. 706.

"wakeful anguish": John Keats, *The Complete Poems of John Keats*
    (New York: Modern Library, 1994), p. 194.

THE FLY

"Seest thou . . . loins of Albion": *CPP*, p. 114.

SPIRITUAL WARFARE

"I . . . drew out several neighbours": *CPP*, p. 732.

"all soldiers . . . slaves": *Blake Records*, p. 125.

"Bow of burning gold . . . pleasant Land": *CPP*, p. 96.

"solid without . . . without pain": *CPP*, p. 71.

"Selfhood . . . Immortal / Spirit": *CPP*, p. 142.

"To hinder another . . . Negative is Vice": *CPP*, p. 601.

"Spirit by self-examination . . . Life": *CPP*, p. 142.

"The most sublime . . . before you": *CPP*, p. 36.

WORK

"I never . . . ill or not": Gilchrist, p. 259.

"Turn . . . artist": Ackroyd, p. 313.

"Exuberance . . . beauty": *CPP*, p. 38.

"*Energy* . . . delight": *CPP*, p. 34.

"he who . . . breeds pestilence": *CPP*, p. 35.

"not because . . . Understandings": *CPP*, p. 564.

"sooner murder . . . unacted desires": *CPP*, p. 38.

"Mere enthusiasm . . . in all": *CPP*, p. 645.

"Passion . . . Beauty Itself": *CPP*, p. 653.

"The Desire of Man . . . Infinite": *CPP*, p. 3.

"lifelong career . . . Lakeside poets": Ackroyd, p. 41.

ETERNITY

"Wheel within . . . peace": *CPP*, p. 159.

"wheel without . . . each other": *CPP*, p. 159.

"Period . . . is Done": *CPP*, p. 127.

"Eternal Now": *CPP*, p. 592.

"pulsation": *CPP*, p. 127.

"Satan . . . find": *CPP*, p. 136.

"is the sensory . . . we aren't": Tom Wolfe, *The Electric Kool-Aid Acid Test* (New York: Picador, 2008), p. 144.

"There are historical . . . first of all": Wolfe, p. 144.

"but he's still . . . emotions don't": Wolfe, p. 145.

"flow": Mihaly Csikszentmihalyi, *The Flow: The Psychology of Optimal Experience* (New York: Harper Perennial Modern Classics, 2008).

"My Fairy . . . Europe": *CPP*, p. 60.

"When I am . . . then published": *The Portable William Blake*, ed. Alfred Kazin (New York: Penguin, 1977), p. 691.

"[t]his Poem . . . Public": *CPP*, p. 730.

"I have written . . . Labor or Study": *CPP*, p. 729.

DICTATION

"The more . . . other will recede": Eugen Herrigel, *Zen in the Art of Archery*, trans. R. F. C. Hull (London: Routledge and Kegan Paul, 1953), pp. 46–47.

"If the . . . go out": *CPP*, p. 494.

"poetry . . . at all": John Keats, *The Selected Letters of John Keats*, ed. Grant F. Scott (Cambridge, MA: Harvard University Press, 2005), p. 57.

"Do you . . . a soul?": Keats, *Letters*, p. 291.

"He who would . . . into flying": Friedrich Nietzsche, *The Portable Nietzsche*, ed. and trans. Walter Kaufmann (New York: Penguin, 1977), p. 307.

THE FOURFOLD

"Mutual Forgiveness . . . Paradise": *CPP*, p. 259.

"each shall . . . good": *CPP*, p. 139.

"Now I fourfold . . . Newtons sleep": *CPP*, p. 722.

"A frowning Thistle . . . my way": *CPP*, p. 721.

"Earth was not . . . eternal life sprung": *CPP*, p. 71.

"More! More! . . . satisfy Man": *CPP*, p. 2.

"the road . . . palace of wisdom": *CPP*, p. 35.

"you never . . . more than enough": *CPP*, p. 37.

"Enough! Or Too Much!": *CPP*, p. 38.

INFINITE WRITING

"If a thing . . . infinite": *CPP*, p. 604.

"God keep me . . . Patience": Herman Melville, *Moby-Dick; or, The Whale* (New York: Penguin, 2002), p. 157.

"Finite . . . Venture": Dickinson, *Poems*, p. 403.

"an unsatisfied . . . often is": C. S. Lewis, *Surprised by Joy: The Shape of my Early Life* (New York: Houghton Mifflin Harcourt, 1995), pp. 15–16.

"unnameable something . . . falling waves": C. S. Lewis, *The Pilgrim's Regress* (London: Eerdman's Pocket Edition, 1981), p. 204.